Unpacking Faith

Unpacking Faith

A Resource for Catholic Military Connected Adolescents and their Parents

Mark T. Moitoza

A gift to the Military Ministry at St. Peter Channel. Keep sharing the faith!

Mark T. Moitoza

Cloverdale Books
South Bend

Unpacking Faith: A Resource for Catholic Military Connected
Adolescents and their Parents

Mark T. Moitoza

Published by
Cloverdale Books
An Imprint of Cloverdale Corporation
South Bend, Indiana 46601
www.CloverdaleBooks.com

Library of Congress Cataloging-in-Publication Data
Moitoza, Mark T.
  Unpacking faith : a resource for Catholic military connected adolescents and their
parents / Mark T. Moitoza.
     p. cm.
  Summary: "Unpacking Faith offers reflections for military connected youth and
parents to discuss the challenges of transition in the context of the Catholic faith.
The book focuses on how we live, move, and have our being in Christ. Each section
in this resource has reflection questions, applications, and questions to foster
dialogue between youth and parent"--Provided by publisher.
  Includes bibliographical references.
  ISBN-13: 978-1-929569-34-2 (pbk.)
  ISBN-10: 1-929569-34-3 (pbk.)
  1. Parent and teenager--Religious aspects--Catholic Church. 2. Children of military
personnel. I. Title.

  BX2352.M58 2007
  248.8'3--dc22

                              2007020894

Cover incorporates original photography of artwork created by Martin Mayer –
Bronze figure Jakobs Pilgrim on the Maximilianstrasse in Speyer, Germany.

Excerpts from the English translation of The Roman Missal ©1973, International
Committee on English in the Liturgy, Inc. (ICEL). All rights reserved.

Printed in the United States of America
on recycled paper made from 100% post-consumer waste

For my parents, Ed and Joan,
in gratitude for the many ways they move me
by sharing their faith, asking questions
and listening well.

Father, all powerful and ever-living God,
we do well always and everywhere to give you thanks.

In you we live and move and have our being.
Each day you show us a Father's love; your Holy Spirit,
dwelling within us, gives us on earth the hope of unending joy.

Your gift of the Spirit,
who raised Jesus from the dead,
is the foretaste and promise
of the pascal feast of heaven.

With thankful praise,
in company with the angels,
we glorify the wonders of your power:

Holy, holy, holy...[1]

> Preface of Sundays in Ordinary Time VI
> The pledge of an eternal Easter

---

[1] *Roman Catholic Sacramentary*, (The Catholic Book Publishing Company, Totowa, NJ, 1985), Preface of Sundays in Ordinary Time VI, The pledge of an eternal Easter. Original text found in The Roman Missal, 1972, International Committee on English in the Liturgy, Inc. (ICEL).

Table of Contents

Preface

Unpacking Faith: A Resource for Catholic Military Connected Adolescents and their Parents is designed to guide high school youth to discover how their Catholic identity contributes to an awareness of self in their transient lifestyle.

Military life is filled with many transitions. For a long time growing up in the military has meant moving every few years while also dealing with friends and mentors moving throughout each assignment too. Currently, the reality of multiple and extended deployments has increased the frequency and stress of transitions on family life. As a young person moves through adolescence they begin to ponder their own identity as they strive to move toward a sense of self. Without a home town or a specific place to call home, military connected youth confront the search of identity along with the challenges of rootlessness and restlessness.

There are many resources designed to help guide young people through a search for understanding the self. Unfortunately, most of them assume the constant of a nurturing community grounded in a specific location. This faith resource specifically deals with the frequency, multiplicity and pastoral issues that are present in the mobile life that military connected families confront today.

Unpacking Faith holds up the model of pilgrimage as a basic tool for unpacking a sense of identity grounded in faith. A pilgrim seeks union with God as he or she transitions from place to place. The Catholic faith provides models for living that help military connected Catholic youth self-reflect based on the love of God in their lives. The sacramental life provides physical markers of encounters with Christ through experience, location, feeling, and memory.

Two of the important constants in this transient lifestyle remain faith and family. Each section in this resource has reflections along with ideas for applying those reflections (in the form of exercises, prayers and activities). Each section also has questions to foster dialogue between youth and parent. The resource may be used while a parent is deployed allowing parents to stay connected via e-mail or phone calls to the deeper questions while they are away.

Military connected Catholic youth are seeking to make sense of their lives. The three sections in this resource highlight the many ways that God lives in them, moves in them and has being in them (Acts 17:28). Each section breaks open experiences that provide faith connections. This process unpacks the consistent areas of the mobile life that encourage change, growth and reflection which moves the adolescent toward a grater understanding of self.

1
Introduction

Military connected youth and their families are familiar with frequent change. Packing up, saying goodbye, moving to a new location, unpacking and starting over again becomes a repetitive ritual. There is, among military families, a desire to set roots along with a certain realization that change will soon happen again. This mobile lifestyle is full of flux and tension which create awkward moments where one can feel totally unconnected.

One of the most common experiences among military connected youth is found in a simple question. That question is 'Where are you from?' This simple, normal conversation-starting question causes many military connected youth to pause, stumble and even make answers up. The challenge of finding a place, in a mysterious way, also presents a gift. Military connected youth have the opportunity to be true pilgrims that allows them to find their identity beyond the boundaries of location. This way of life is not easy but the ability to experience God throughout the world is a gift.

This gift from God can be missed if we never unpack our experiences. We can move from place to place gathering and packing up experiences. If we do not also take the time to unpack those experiences then we miss the opportunity to make connections or reflect upon the many ways that we have encountered the love of Christ. This resource offers ideas to open up and embrace our collected experiences. As pilgrims we have experienced the love of Christ through the people we met, the creation we played on, and within the spiritual growth that took place in our lives.

Growing up Catholic in a military connected family offers three gifts that will be examined throughout this resource. They include the gifts of living, moving and being. First, as Catholics we are connected to people around the world that pray, celebrate and live the faith throughout the rhythm of the liturgical season. We are also connected to a wide variety of relationships that give us life. Second, through our faith we move and are moved. In fact, we grow in the sacramental life from the very moment we put on Christ represented in the white garment of our baptism. We renew that commitment to be moved and changed every time we participate in the celebration of the Eucharist. Finally, for as much as we might desire things to stay the same so that we can just be, we discover that through our very being we change. That change comes from our many experiences especially those that we encounter in prayer.

As a military connected youth I remember many rituals that my parents shared to help me and my siblings stay connected. When we were young moving into a new home was something of an adventure. There were new rooms to explore, the expectation of our household goods (familiar stuff) arriving, the experience of camping indoors among half unpacked boxes and things that needed to be put together or put away. My mom often gave my brother and me the task of peeling off the moving tags on all of our furniture. The incentive was a nickel per tag. We would race around our new home looking for as many moving tags as we could. Some tags were in plain sight on the front of a headboard, some were hidden behind the back leg of a kitchen chair. No matter how hard we searched there usually were a few missed tags that would be found from the previous move. We could always spot those because they were a different color or from a different moving company. They were also more difficult to remove because they had been stuck for so long. Hunting for moving tags kept us busy and probably kept us out of the way a bit. We loved it though because we were involved. At the end of the search we cashed in our tags with high hopes for the many ways that we could spend the change.

My parents cultivated our skills to help us embrace the transitions of a military connected family. When we learned about a new assignment we often did research about the place we were moving to. Our travels from place to place would include stops where the whole family could have fun. Faith was important to my parents. They shared their gifts in a variety of ways at each assignment. They often asked us questions about the homilies we had just heard. Their questions not only encouraged us to pay attention but more importantly they got us to talk about applying faith in our daily lives. We developed family traditions like inviting people far away from home to our table for Thanksgiving and one of my favorites, fondue on Christmas Eve.

In the 26 years that my father served in the United States Air Force there were many challenges and there were many opportunities for joy too. With all of the moving and transitions that military connected families experience there are some constants that are so much a part of who we are that we sometimes forget that they even exist. Our family and our faith remain with us wherever we move. This does not mean that they don't change and grow; in fact, they evolve and develop sometimes faster than we are aware. These intimate relationships, however, are the ones that know our life story and encourage it. They know where we are from and where we might be heading.

These intimate relationships; the ones we have with our parents, our immediate family and God, are integral to our story. Each one of us has a story to tell. It is as basic as the number of homes we have lived in or the number of schools we have attended. It is also as complicated as watching our own parents deal with stress as, at the same time, we all say goodbye to the people and places that have become important to us and prepare for the unknown of a new assignment, a new home and a new school. Unpacking our faith means taking the time to look back at both the basic and the complicated experiences.

This resource is designed especially for Catholic military connected adolescents and their parents. It examines what it means to grow up Catholic in a military connected family. Our Catholic faith provides a foundation that enables us to connect all of our lived experiences. Our faith truly is built upon the meaning of Catholicism defined as universal because we have had the opportunity to experience the Catholic faith throughout our own country and for many of us in foreign lands too.

As military connected parents and youth reflect, journal and share their thoughts a deeper understanding of the pilgrim faith is embraced and encouraged. Stepping back and reflecting upon our life transitions allows us to really see the many ways that Christ has lived and moved and remains present in our lives. These reflections demand a sense of maturity and respect. If we are truly open to God's presence in our lives we will notice that God has indeed been present through it all. It may appear that things have happened by coincidence. The lived experience, however, highlights again and again that Christ has put people in our lives or has put us in the lives of others beyond the rationality of coincidence.

Military connected families are familiar with packing up and preparing for a change. This resource invites you to slow down a bit, to unpack some things, to spend some time exploring, to look at where Christ has been and continues to be present in your life. It also invites you to remember that you are not alone. Over 5% of the U.S. population grew up in a U.S. military connected family.[2] Roughly speaking about 25% of the population in the U.S. military identifies themselves as Catholic. These statistics are important on two fronts. First, we probably often think that there are not too many people who understand what it is like to live a life on the move. Yet a large number of people have had similar experiences. Second is the reality that as a Catholic you are, by virtue of your baptism, a member of the Catholic Church that deeply cares about you. There are people around the world praying for you and your family.

During the Liturgy of the Eucharist there are several prefaces in the Catholic mass which precede the Eucharistic Prayer. The sixth preface, a choice for Sundays in ordinary time, is very appropriate for military connected youth and families. In that preface we hear the words found in the Acts of the Apostles chapter seventeen, verse twenty-eight.

In him we live and move and have our being...[3]

Scripture scholars point out that these words from Acts, in the New Testament, indicate that the missionary Paul used language to help the early believers in Athens grapple with the truth that God, as a creator, is a giver rather than a receiver. This was an important challenge in the early church where believers thought that they had to bring offerings to the place where God dwelled represented by various idols. Paul's sermon was designed to help them and us recognize that God dwells beyond boundaries and seasons.[4] It is my conviction that this phrase, that comes from the early Christians trying to figure out what faith was all about, applies very well to those of us growing up in military connected families. As we pray these words we are reminded to celebrate the gift of pilgrimage that God has given us and our families. We recall the gift of faith (the recognition of God's presence) which travels with us as we move into a new community and attempt to discover our way. That same gift of faith guides us when, once again, we have to say goodbye. As we make our way the gift of faith encourages us to be grateful for the places, experiences, and people that God has graced us with.

This resource is designed in three parts based upon the verse from the Acts of the Apostles (17:28): *Live, Move, and Being.* Each part has four reflections that offer insights, connections and new ways of seeing the life and spirituality of a military connected adolescent. In the *Live* section we examine relationship connections by looking at our life story, our family, our sacramental life, and the ways that we may discover our giftedness. In the *Move* section we examine faith connections by looking at saying goodbye well, noticing how God moves us, recognizing how the movement of deployments affects our lives, and understanding what it means to move with faith. Finally, in the *Being* section we examine our relationship with Christ by looking at the ways we recognize Christ's presence, the ways in which we pray our experiences, what it means to be a disciple of Christ and how we are all called to be Christ for one another.

You may choose to read one reflection a week. It could be a resource for you to use as your family moves over the summer months. You might choose to pick one reflection at a time based upon how it speaks out to you. Finally, you might want to spend time with these reflections while your parent is deployed. In fact, you and your deployed parent might agree to work on this project together while you are apart. You can e-mail answers and questions to one another during the deployment or plan to revisit them when your parent returns.

Pilgrimage

In many faiths there is a tradition of going on pilgrimage. A person leaves home and goes on a journey seeking out God. This journey is different than going on a trip or a vacation. For the tourist, going on vacation, the whole point is focused on getting away from the daily schedule and escaping to the destination. For the pilgrim the entire process of the journey is what matters. It is the preparation, the struggle to get there and multiple experiences along the way that makes up a pilgrimage.

Throughout the middle ages there are many stories of pilgrims in Europe that traveled from cathedral to cathedral making their way from place to place and back again. In Speyer, Germany there is a beautiful Romanesque Cathedral (Kaiserdom) built near the Rhine River. In recognition of the many pilgrims that made their way through Speyer, the Diocese of Speyer gave the town a statue of a pilgrim on their main street (Maximillianstrasse). It is one of my favorite statues because there is so much to notice in this simple pilgrim. The statue depicts a man who looks tired. He has a simple shawl and hat to keep him warm. He is carrying a very small bag of possessions on his back and has a walking stick. Most noticeable though are his feet. He is not wearing shoes or socks. His feet appear bigger than they should be, making you wonder if the difficulties of the pilgrimage are worth it. Yet, there is something that encourages him to move on. This specific statue shows the pilgrim with his back to the cathedral. He is leaving Speyer implying that he had made his visit and was pursuing the next holy place on his pilgrimage.

I like this pilgrim statue because it reminds me that even through tough times and struggles there are reasons to have hope. A pilgrimage is a challenge but no pilgrim is ever alone. This pilgrim doesn't carry much because part of the journey relies on trusting in the providence of God. God will provide for the needs of the pilgrim. The closest thing we have in the Catholic world today to a pilgrimage is the international gathering known as World Youth Day begun by Pope John Paul II. Millions of youth and young adults have gathered together over the years from around the world to be others and celebrate the Catholic faith. The travel itself is challenging and yet the opportunity for rejoicing in God's loving presence renews faith so much that these pilgrims return to share the gifts that they have been blessed with.

A military connected family that moves frequently is on a life-long pilgrimage. They move about the country or the world. They notice different ways of living, unique traditions, creative customs and festivals. A military connected adolescent has the opportunity to see the many faces of God which is a gift to be celebrated.

Deployments

This resource would not be complete if it did not acknowledge the reality of deployments in military life today. In the spring of 2003 I was serving as a Catholic youth ministry leader at the U.S. Army Post in Heidelberg, Germany. Watching the military prepare for the war in Iraq reminded many of why men and women in uniform train so hard all year long. At a moment's notice everyone in uniform knew what to do to move the mission forward. Families, however, dealt with the pre-deployment, deployment and post-deployment experiences in lots of different ways.

I learned about some of the reality of deployments through the eyes of military connected young people and their families as well as friends I had who were sent to Iraq and Afghanistan. My experience is honestly at least one step removed. My Dad had a remote assignment to Thailand when I was three years old. I remember getting my first letter from him. I also remember listening to cassette tapes he sent to us. The reality is that most of my memories of that time come through pictures and stories that my parents have told me as I grew up.

Teenagers growing up in military families today are dealing with a lot especially when the prospect of extended and multiple deployments are thrust upon their family life. While deep down they understand that their parent is serving a mission to promote peace there is a definitive loss that takes place when one or sometimes two members of the family are deployed.

Most caring adults want to do whatever they can to help young people survive the trying times of deployment. Often the military tries to develop programs to alleviate or solve problems. Young people that have a parent deployed do need caring people to listen. They are not so much interested in programs to solve their issues though. What they crave the most are people who can identify with their experiences. They really want to share thoughts and feelings with someone who has had similar experiences and knows what it is like to have a parent deployed in today's military. The Military Family Institute at Purdue University published a helpful report in 2005 called *Adjustments among Adolescents in Military Families When a Parent Is Deployed.* Some of the highlights of this report, from interviews with adolescents who had a parent deploy, showed that teenagers demonstrated great maturity and a willingness to take on additional responsibilities. Their social life and school life, however, tended to experience a decline due to depressed feelings, increased responsibilities and a fear of reading the paper or watching the news. [5]

Pre-deployment finds the family getting ready for the day that a big change will occur. Once the deployed parent has gone the family has to adjust to a new way of living. The parent who left is also making adjustments while their family support system remains at home. There is a period of waiting and wondering. Is the deployed parent safe? Will they try to call or chat online today? How are we going to handle the daily issues that occur? Finally, there is the reality of the post-deployment when a parent returns and somehow has to reintegrate into a family system that has evolved and changed. It takes time to readjust and figure out how the reunited family dynamic is going to play out.

Deployments are like a pilgrimage of sorts because both the deployed parent and the family that remains home journey to new places. The entire family experiences new ways of being while they are apart. For many, the deployment can become a time which renews their prayer life. Prayer can become a place to reunite with your loved one and Christ. There is a reflection in this resource about deployments which offers some ideas that may be helpful for dealing with the challenges of this new way of living. It highlights the need to self-reflect, to develop life skills, and to acknowledge that new experiences will bring a variety of complex emotional issues throughout the deployment process.

Catholic military connected youth

There is something unique about your life that has the potential to create passion for both discovery and wonder. Because of your experiences you will be able to help build bridges of understanding in the world. You move because your parent or parents have chosen to serve their country. The challenges and struggles that you face represent some of the many ways that you too serve your country.

I am convinced that being Catholic and growing up in the military offers a unique perspective that helps us understand our mobile lifestyle as a pilgrimage. While we long for what we don't have, permanence and familiarity, we cultivate new ways of living and discovering. To be sure, there are many things that are difficult about moving and having a parent or two in uniform. The gifts we discover along the way, however, present opportunities for great joy.

This resource is developed with you in mind. It encourages you to create a map of understanding which you can reference throughout your life. It also points to a path of *being* wherever it is that God moves you. The activities, journal questions and reflections are designed to help you unpack what you have picked up along the way. You are encouraged to share these thoughts and reflections with your parent(s). You might be able to do that across the kitchen table or on a walk that you take together. You also might be able to go through this experience while your parent is deployed. You could share thoughts through e-mail, phone calls or even prepare a way to share when your parent returns.

As a Catholic growing up in the military you are a part of the Archdiocese for the Military Services, USA. There are over 1.4 million Catholic men, women and children that belong to the Military Archdiocese. Each Catholic chaplain in the U.S. military is endorsed by the Military Archdiocese. If you celebrated a sacrament in a military chapel, like baptism or confirmation, the sacramental record is kept on file in the offices of the Military Archdiocese in Washington, D.C. No matter where your family is assigned you are a member of the Catholic Church. The church needs your presence, your gifts and above all your unique view of living as a pilgrim. I hope that the resource helps you to unfold your story so that you may confidently share your gifts knowing that you are a child of God.

Catholic military connected parents

As a military connected youth I gained much wisdom from my parents who were willing to share their experiences. When I was thirteen years old my family was preparing to move to Europe for the first time. Many of our relatives told my parents what a great experience it would be for their children. My mother responded by saying that it would also be a great experience for them too. This small phrase helped me to remember that we traveled together as a family and shared many experiences along the way.

The gift of being able to ask questions and listen well is vitally important to parents in the military. I am not sure how my parents survived setting up so many homes and starting so many new jobs while trying to also make sure that we were connected in our new communities. I do, however, believe that our Catholic faith provided more than a touchstone of stability. My parents got involved in Catholic faith communities wherever they lived which in turn involved us too. Our faith helped us as a family to navigate, connect, belong, rejoice, mourn, and hope.

Recently, the National Study of Youth and Religion noted that throughout the United States adults today do not spend much time talking to their adolescents about faith. The study also noted that teens today are not the same spiritual seekers of previous generations. Teenagers today value and respect the religious practices of their parents.[6] The influence of parents cannot be understated when it comes to the lives of their teenager(s). Parents who take the time to practice their faith and share what it means encourage their children to become active, reflective and holy young people.

Unpacking Faith invites you to reflect on your experiences of the mobile lifestyle with your child. Some parents in the military were military connected youth themselves and can identify well with some of the issues. Other parents did not move when they grew up and so the frequent changes are new transitions for everyone in the family. Either way your love as a parent paves the path for your child to grow. This resource is designed for both of you to read on your own and then share thoughts later. Each section has stories, activities and reflections. Your own commitment to spend time reflecting on these sections will set a tone that your child will follow. Your willingness to listen without always having the answer will also enable an opportunity to talk and question together. Take advantage of the things you may not know to start a shared project with your child and research the answer together. Your combined curiosity might lead you to fill in missing pieces of your family history, to discover an answer to a question about the Catholic faith, or even to uncover why your family moved to one military installation rather than another.

One of the major themes of the National Study of Youth Religion highlights the realization that religious practices appear to play an important role in the faith life of adolescents today.[7] Belonging to a family that serves others through their vocation in the armed forces is a great starting point. Adolescents of this current generation, as noted previously, follow the spiritual and faith practices of their parents. Your example of living and practicing the Catholic faith is the most important influence you can have on your child. To spend time embracing the possibility of exploring new spiritual practices with your teenager will become a gift to be cherished.

Finally, you should know that you are not alone. As a Catholic in the military you are a part of the Archdiocese for the Military Services, USA. There are over 1.4 million Catholic men, women and children that belong to the Military Archdiocese. Each Catholic chaplain in the U.S. military is endorsed by the Military Archdiocese. If your family celebrated a sacrament in a military chapel, like baptism, confirmation, or marriage the sacramental record is kept on file in the offices of the Military Archdiocese in Washington, D.C. When a Catholic civilian moves from one state to another they also change dioceses. A diocese is a territorial area with a bishop that serves as the shepherd. The bishop leads by helping the community of faith to provide for the needs of Catholics in that area. The Archdiocese for the Military Services, USA is a non-territorial archdiocese with an archbishop and three auxiliary bishops. Their pastoral responsibility reaches wherever members of the military and their families are assigned. I hope that this resource helps you to unfold your story so that you may confidently share your gifts knowing that you also are a child of God.

Chapter 1 Notes

[2] Donna Musil, *Brats Our Journey: Our Journey Home*, (Brats Without Borders, Inc., Eatonton, Georgia), 2005.

[3] *The Roman Missal*, 1973, Preface of Sundays in Ordinary Time IV.

[4] Raymond Brown, et. al., The New Jerome Biblical Commentary, (Prentice Hall, Upper Saddle River, New Jersey, 1990), 725.

[5] Angela J. Huebner, Ph.D. and Jay A. Mancini, Ph.D., *Adjustments among Adolescents in Military Families When a Parent Is Deployed*, (Final Report to the Military Family Research Institute and Department of Defense Quality of Life Office, June 30, 2005), 5-6. This study notes both the issues of risk and resilience that confront youth when a parent is deployed.

[6] Christian Smith with Melinda Lundquist Denton, *Soul Searching: The Religious and Spiritual Lives of American Teenagers*, (Oxford University Press, New York, New York), 2005, 115. Parents of teenagers appear to play an important role in the character of their children's lives. In the immediacy of parenting teenagers, parents may feel a loss of control and influence over their teens, but nationally representative statistics show that the religious practices and commitments of parents remain an important influence on the religious practices and commitments of teenage children. Family socialization generally seems to work when it comes to teenagers' religious faith and practice. Furthermore, the quality of relationships that parents build with their teenagers and their own choices about marriage relationships, education, and occupation-insofar as they have choices in these areas-also create family contexts that again form the outcome of their teenagers' religious and spiritual lives. © *Soul Searching: The Religious and Spiritual Lives of American Teenagers* (2005) by Christian Smith, By permission of Oxford University Press

[7] Ibid, Christian Smith. For the committed adolescent, religion is not simply a matter of general identity or affiliation or cognitive belief. Faith for these

teenagers is also *activated, practiced, and formed* through specific religious and spiritual practices. For such teens, faith involves their intentionally engaging in regularly enacted religious habits and works that have theological, spiritual, or moral meanings that form their lives, such as habitually worshipping with other believers, reading scriptures, praying regularly, practicing confession and forgiveness and reconciliation, engaging in service to others, using one's body in particular ways, tuning into religious music and other religious art forms, and engaging in regular faith education and formation, 27 (italics original). © *Soul Searching: The Religious and Spiritual Lives of American Teenagers* (2005) by Christian Smith, By permission of Oxford University Press

2
ƉIVE:
Connecting Relationships

In him we live. Our first relationship begins with God who created us in his image and likeness[8]. We are born to parents who love us. They nurture us and help us to differentiate from right and wrong. They share their faith with us through their practice and through the ways they talk about faith. For military connected youth it is easy to feel unconnected. When we do feel unconnected it is important to take time to acknowledge where we come from and to recognize those that encourage our growth. The next four reflections are designed to help you begin unpacking your experiences of faith, people, and places and like the pilgrim, to take a look at what has happened along the way.

My life up to now:
So where are you from anyway?

Can you remember the last time someone asked you 'Where are you from?' It seems like such a simple question but for many military connected youth there is no easy answer. When a young person in a military connected family is asked this simple question there is often a long silent pause. The pause is not because we have something to hide but rather the pause highlights the reality of the unknown.

While growing up in a military connected family you may have been born on or near a U.S. military installation that your parent(s) was assigned to. After a couple of years your family likely moved to another place. This pattern would normally continue every two or three years. A typical 15 year old could easily have lived in at least seven different places. Sound familiar?

This is exactly where the struggle lies for military connected youth. Do we say that we are from the place we were born? We often have no memory of that place. Do we say we are from the place(s) our parents are from? This offers a sense of connection but also serves as a reminder that we ourselves do not have a hometown to return to, a place to be recognized or even a community that is familiar to us. Finally, do we say we are from the place that we are currently living? This also presents problems because although it is probably the most accurate answer for the moment, the location may not necessarily resonate with the place that we consider home. In fact, we will probably move from that place within a year or so.

New homes, new schools, new communities, new friends, and new structures to navigate through all represent pieces of the challenges and the gifts of military life. That in itself is complicated enough. Recently, however, the engagement in conflict in the Persian Gulf has forced military connected families to endure the reality of extended and multiple deployments which come with a whole set of different challenges.

⊃Reflection Questions
My life up to now

- Where were you born?

- Where do you live now?

- What do you say to people when they ask 'Where are you from?'

- If you could pick a place to be from, where would it be?

- What do you like about moving frequently?

- What is challenging about moving frequently?

- How has your parent(s) helped you prepare for a move?

➲Activity
My life up to now

While visiting Catholic youth in military communities I often share my life story. Of course, that scares a lot of people because they think I am going to go on and on. I surprise the groups, however, by instead mapping all of the places I have lived which takes less than five minutes. My last name has a Portuguese origin. I like to think that I am connected somehow to the culture of the great navigators of Portugal. Because of that history I really like maps. When read correctly, maps can be a useful tool to find out where we are going and how we are going to get there. Maps also identify the uniqueness of a starting point which may include mountains, rivers, forests or deserts. A map can give a sense of direction.

In mapping my own life story I connect the dots from each military installation that my family lived at. This new map gives a framework to my life story that I can see and that I can show others. It allows me to begin to trace the pilgrimage that God has given to me and my family (see the Map it Out activity on page 24.)

➲Map It Out[9]

- Take some time to map out your life story and create your own map.

- On a blank sheet of paper draw an outline of all of the continents you have lived on.

- Mark the place you were born.

- Mark all of the places you have lived.

- Now trace a line from mark to mark in the order of the places you have lived.

- Take a look at your pilgrimage map.

- What do you notice?

- What do you know about the place you were born?

- Do any of the lines overlap or crisscross?

- Where have you enjoyed living the most?

- What is the one place you couldn't wait to get out of?

- How many homes have you lived in on this pilgrimage up to now?

- How many times were you the new person in school?

So there it is. You now have a map that outlines where you were born and where you have been. The outline, however, is only the surface of your story. Each of those locations and the trips that took you from place to place are packed with experiences. Actually, there are stories of faith and hope that even precede our birth. There are also, as we will see, stories of faith and hope in our map that point us to the kingdom of heaven.

⮎Teen and Parent Conversation
My life up to now

Share your thoughts with one another based on the following questions.

Teen

- What surprised you about mapping out your life story?

- What is one story of a place or person that you recalled from drawing your map?

- How do you answer those that ask you where are you from?

Parent

- How is your life as a parent in the military different from your own childhood?

- Tell a story about the birth of your child and what it was like to bring them home.

- How do you find healthy ways to handle the stress of moving?

Our Family:
Where do we really come from?

All of my relatives grew up in Newport and Middletown, Rhode Island. I was born at the Newport Naval hospital and have tried all my life to claim Rhode Island as the place that I am from. Several weeks after I was born, however, we moved to Nellis Air Force Base in Las Vegas, Nevada. My military connected family was on the go, moving every few years. We would often visit our cousins in Rhode Island which was for me always a great time to look forward to. It also, however, served as a reminder of what I didn't have. I remember cousins who were in high school with classmates they knew from first grade. I recall walking into stores where my parents were recognized and called by name even though they hadn't been there in fifteen years. I was born in Rhode Island but I wasn't really from there.

Spending time with my extended family helped me to realize, in some part, that where I do come from is not so much a place but a culture. Visiting relatives gave me the opportunity to learn about my parents' and grandparents' stories. Over the past few years my parents have begun to record a family genealogy. Like a map, this outline helps us to see connections that were not always so clear.

If we think about it, most people living in the United States have family that came from somewhere else over the past 300 years or so. We often think that people that grow up in one place have it made because they know where they are rooted. If we uncover records of their family history though we can see that they can also create a life map which depicts a journey from or to a foreign land.

I mentioned before that my last name is Portuguese. My great grandparents came from two islands in the Azores: Faial and San Miguel. My mother's family is Irish and French Canadian. I loved visiting my Grandparents not only to learn how my parents grew up but also to understand where my grandparents' families came from and how they got there. I learned from them how they relied on family and friends to make it through times of challenge and suffering. I also learned, from these visits, how important it was to gather with family and friends to celebrate key moments in life. In looking back at my own family history I am able to uncover a sense of self. Our culture is a core part of who we are. It is through our culture that we relate to God, celebrate things that matter and share food around the table.

I have found growing up in a military connected family that our cultures can often become intertwined. My parents grew up with a deeper sense of their culture since they experienced ways that those cultures were celebrated and expressed. Military connected youth grow up in both the military culture and a mixed experience of collected cultures gathered from the many places they have lived. We know how to speak in acronyms and understand that the military has a mission that requires the focus and energy of those on active duty. Military culture becomes a part of who we are but it is not our entire identity. We are, in a sense, piecing parts of our cultures together. If we could represent it accurately it would probably look a lot like a modern stained glass window. That view, through which we see the world, grows and changes with each new culture and place that we have lived.

➲Reflection Questions
Our Family

- Where were your parents born?

- Where were your grandparents born?

- What countries did your ancestors come from?

- Can you uncover when your ancestors arrived in the United States of America?

- What do you know about the faith experiences and practices of your extended family?

- What can you do to learn more about the culture(s) that your family comes from?

- What have you learned about yourself by discovering your heritage?

➲Activity
Our Family

The Irish love to tell stories. Sometimes they stretch the truth and can be accused of having a bit of the blarney in them. This storytelling, however, enables the Irish to hold onto the things that are important by re-telling the stories of their culture that matter. The Portuguese have a word, *saudade*, which refers to something that one longs for. It is difficult to translate. *Saudade* points to a sense of something lost that cannot be regained for a long time; it is an experience of loss and hope combined together. It is a mood that permeates the culture through a melancholy attitude. In some strange way the combination of these cultures has created in me a desire to uncover our story of family history while at the same time looking ahead.

In the last session you were encouraged to create a map of places you have lived. You are now invited to add to that outline by extending your story to include your family history.

⮕Family Tree

- Draw the outlines of the countries your family come from somewhere on your map.

- Add the names of your parents and grandparents in these countries since they carry part of that culture and share it with you.

- Write down one or two customs that your family holds on to from its' cultures (it may be stories, food, celebrations, prayers, etc,)

- If you could visit one of these countries what would you most like to see or experience?

- What traditions does your immediate family have that come from your cultural background?

So now your map has some history. You come from a family that has probably traveled from somewhere else. In their desire to stay rooted to their home they hold on to some of their cultural traditions. Undoubtedly, they also developed some of their own traditions. All of this is a part of your story. It is, in a sense, where you really come from. Each of us has a cultural background that influences us in some ways. Our military connected families also have the benefit of living in the military culture that moves us to many different places. Each of these places offers their own cultural input if we are brave enough to venture outside of the installation gate to experience new things.

It is often said that with privilege comes responsibility. We have been given the gift to experience and live in multiple cultures. This is true even if we have lived in different parts of the United States. We have come to know that there are different ways of doing things and different ways of viewing the world. Our cross cultural experiences sometimes help us to translate for others. Often those that live in one place hold tightly to their way of life. When new people enter the community their customs and traditions are viewed as foreign or even wrong. Your mobile lifestyle has given you the gift to observe and appreciate different ways of being. Your responsibility comes in the form of speaking up for those who are misunderstood. By being a bridge builder between cultures you have the ability to encourage others to cross the bridge of understanding. Helping others see differences as differences rather than identifying particular customs as right and wrong points to the multifaceted face of God we spoke about in the Introduction.

⮑Teen and Parent Conversation
Our Family

Share your thoughts with one another based on the following questions.

Teen

- What's one thing you would really like to know about one of your cultures?

- What are the new traditions that your family has developed?

- Look up the meaning of *saudade* online. What words or traditions are unique to your cultural background?

Parent

- What traditions from your childhood do you miss now that you move frequently?

- What is one thing about your cultural background that bothers you? Why?

- How can your family add traditions from the various assignments they have experienced?

Our Sacramental Life:
At home in Christ

As a Catholic family growing up in the military can, on the surface, appear like a disjointed experience. The transitions that happen all year long just add to the normal changes of a new assignment. Friends move throughout the year, policies change just as we were getting used to them and often expectations change in light of new circumstances or challenges. In the center of all of this movement is our faith life. As Catholics we belong to a sacramental church. The sacraments represent key moments in our lives, where in a community of faith, we encounter Christ. Sacraments serve as reminders that we are not alone.

My experience of the Catholic Church in the U.S. military was a positive one. When our family moved to a new assignment Church was often one of the first places where we felt welcomed. It was almost as if we belonged there even though we had not been there before. Military chapels have a familiar feeling. Maybe it is because these chapels are so simple and basic to allow many different faiths to worship in the same house. As an altar server I remember helping set up the chapel for the Catholic mass. We changed the cross to one with the corpus (body of Jesus) on it. We opened the shutter doors to reveal the Stations of the Cross. In some places we spun out the holy water fonts from the wall near the entrance of the church. We added the things that made this simple church recognizable to Catholics around the world. These familiar symbols and the rituals of the Catholic faith welcomed our family wherever we moved. The celebrations of the sacraments in these many military chapels weave a constant thread of connection through so much moving.

The sacraments help us to connect to the relationships that matter the most; our relationship with Christ, our relationship with family and our relationship with the community. In looking back at my own sacramental life I can identify important experiences that contributed to my life. My baptism was celebrated in the church that my parents were married in Newport, Rhode Island. My first reconciliation and communion were celebrated in the military chapel at Offutt Air Force Base, in Omaha, Nebraska. I received the sacrament of confirmation at the Bitburg Air Base Chapel in Bitburg, Germany. My wife and I were married by a military chaplain in the side chapel of the Kaiserdom in Speyer, Germany and our daughter was baptized in the Patrick Henry Village Chapel in Heidelberg, Germany.

All of these sacramental experiences are special because there are multiple ways to remember them. There is, of course, the location where the sacrament was celebrated sometimes remembered through pictures and stories told to us by our parents. There is the memory of preparing for the sacrament with leaders in the Church who volunteered their time to share the faith. There is the grace-filled moment of the sacrament itself where God's loving embrace welcomes us home and also sends out into the world with a renewed and deeper connection.

As we long to set down roots we do well to follow our desire to reclaim our own story. There are deep connections of Catholicism which contribute to our story. They include:

- a sense of being called
- a relationship with Christ
- a relationship with the Eucharist
- a relationship with the community

These Catholic connections can offer a sense of identity and belonging in our lives as young people growing up in military connected families.

God, who created us, has given each one of us different gifts to share. We are all called by God to serve different needs based on our gifts. God calls us to reach within so that we may go beyond ourselves to serve others. This sense of going home is turned around in faith as we, like the disciples, are called to journey away from home and move past our comfort zones.

Catholics are called to be in relationship with Jesus Christ. Christ understands what it is like to move from place to place. The infant Jesus was born in Bethlehem. He grew up in Nazareth and his public ministry found him moving in and out of many different places. Jesus knew what it was like to say goodbye to good friends and to mourn those who had died. He felt deeply the challenge of not being accepted in his own hometown. The life of Jesus reminds us to give thanks to God for the moments we have with others, however brief they may be. Jesus, in his earthly life, moved in and out of the lives of many people. We have many similarities to share with Christ the Savior who reaches out to us in our daily lives. When we pray we nurture that relationship. When we learn more about our faith our friendship with Christ grows. When we serve others we see the face of Christ in those that need a guiding hand. When we practice our faith by participating in the sacraments and reading the bible we recall that we are created to praise God in a faith-filled community so that we may actually live our faith in the real world with all of its challenges.

Catholics believe in the real presence of Christ in the Eucharist. Each week at the Sunday liturgy we recall the reality that Christ came into the world, died for our sins, and rose from the dead into everlasting life. Our recognition of the real presence of Christ in the Eucharist is a gift that we celebrate throughout our entire life. As Catholics we believe that simple bread and wine in the celebration of the Eucharistic liturgy change into the body and blood of Christ. The Eucharist brings us together. It reminds us where we come from and where we are heading. Actively celebrating the Eucharist reminds us that change is a constant part of life. We are a Eucharistic people. It is what makes us Catholic. Military chapels around the world have Blessed Sacrament chapels where the consecrated host is reserved in a tabernacle. A candle or a light is always lit near the tabernacle to remind us that Christ is present. Christ is our light that helps us find our way in times of change.

We are also in relationship to a community of faith. Our Catholic faith is not something that we celebrate on our own. We gather together to pray for the needs of the entire community, to celebrate with others during the times of joy and to be there for one another during times of loss and transition. A healthy community recognizes one another. Often they know each others names. They pray for one another. They come to lean on each other and offer themselves to be leaned on.

On a Saturday in May 2006 I visited the Catholic faith community at Fort Drum, New York. On the day I arrived everyone on post was hearing the breaking news that a helicopter from the 10th Mountain Division had crashed in Afghanistan and all ten people aboard had died. These ten soldiers were all from Fort Drum. Later that day at the vigil mass the community gathered to pray and to be nourished. It was a powerful experience of prayer. If you didn't know any better you would have thought that you were at a mass for single parents because so many active duty members were deployed. Although the community did not, at the time, know the names of those who had died they prayed for each of them. They prayed for those who would learn the news of the death of their loved one. They prayed that they would continue to be a community of love and support to those who were about to experience loss. They prayed for those who remained on deployment serving in very difficult situations. They prayed to God for hope and strength to go on as they were nourished by a loving community brought together by the Eucharist.

⮌Reflection Questions:
Our Sacramental Life

- Where were you baptized?

- Where did you receive the sacrament of reconciliation and first communion?

- What was one important thing you learned as you prepared for confirmation?

- Who, besides your immediate family, knew about the times you celebrated these sacraments?

- Where did you feel most connected to the Church?

- How does participating in the sacramental life of the Church make a difference in your life?

- How has your community of faith supported those experiencing joy or loss?

➲Activity
Our Sacramental Life

In the last session you were encouraged to add your cultural heritage to your map. This time you are invited to add the faith dimension of your pilgrimage to your life map.

Sacraments

- Draw a symbol of each sacrament you have received near the location you celebrated that sacrament. For example, I received first communion in Omaha, Nebraska so I might draw a cross or a chalice or something that reminds me of that moment near that location.

- Make sure you include symbols for your baptism, first reconciliation, first communion and confirmation. You might also choose to highlight sacraments that other members of your family received.

- Write down the names of godparents and sponsors somewhere on your map.

- Draw a symbol or write a paragraph about what it means for you to join the community of faith each week for the celebration of mass.

- Consider how you would explain the real presence of Christ in the Eucharist to someone who had not heard about that

before? Write down your thoughts about this
question on your map.

So now your map has some sacramental
history. You are a member of the Catholic Church.
Your story of faith is recorded in sacramental
records, in the memory of your family and in the
collective memory of the community where you
received those sacraments. Whatever your location
was or currently is, your faith story is a part of the
faith story of the entire Catholic faith community.
We can dare to say that we are at home in faith
where we encounter God and where God welcomes
wherever we are.

⮕Teen and Parent Conversation
Our Sacramental Life

Share your thoughts with one another based on the following questions.

Teen

- What is something that you specifically remember about one of the sacraments you received?

- What is something about the Catholic faith that you don't quite understand?

- With your parent read through one of the Gospels, (Matthew, Mark, Luke, or John) and map out the many times that Jesus moved in and out of different places throughout his life which began in Bethlehem. You might want to use a bible that has a map of the time of Jesus to help you keep track.

Parent

- Where did you celebrate the sacraments of baptism, first reconciliation, first communion and confirmation?

- When has the community of faith been extremely important to you?

- What is one thing about the Catholic faith that you don't quite understand?

⮎St. Paul

Paul, who used to persecute the early Christians, had an important conversion which influenced the early Church. Saint Paul came to believe that God made salvation available to everyone. This salvation was offered as a free gift and no one could do anything to earn it.[10] Because of his beliefs Saint Paul traveled as a missionary through what is now known as Western Europe and the Middle East. The Catholic Youth Bible has two maps that depict the missionary journeys of Paul.[11]

Saint Paul traveled from place to place. He wrote letters to the early Christian communities explaining what it meant to be a disciple of Christ. Paul was housed, feed and cared for by the local faith communities he visited.

Discovering Giftedness:
Growing in Faith

In the last session we mentioned that God calls us to use our gifts to serve others. But how do we know what gifts or talents we have been given? If I am always moving from place to place how I am supposed to figure them out and then actually start using them? Anything worth discovering takes time. It is the same as we strive to discern our gifts. We learn about our gifts by watching other people use their gifts well and by recognizing the things that we are good at.

A military installation functions like a small town. Everyone has a part to play in order to make things go smoothly. When things don't go smoothly word gets out. Sometimes the small town analogy is a bit too close for comfort when it appears that everyone seems to know what is going on in the lives of others. On the other hand, the small town atmosphere also affords compliments and encouragement. On many military installations young people in Catholic faith communities are teamed up with adult mentors to learn about different ministries in the Church. An adult lector and a youth lector work together to prepare the Sunday readings. The entire community takes notice when a young person reads or serves or does something behind the scenes. Some adults take the time to learn the names of these young people and compliment them when they do something well.

We discover our gifts by practicing different things. By moving around so much we gain access to experience and practice various skills. We may join new activities, explore parts of the world we have never been to, participate in a retreat or meet someone who really likes what they do. We also learn about what we are good at when others recognize us. I have found that the military loves to hand out certificates of recognition. There is something wonderful about this tradition. Time is set aside to recognize that you accomplished something and that your presence made a difference. It is one of the ways that we can learn about our giftedness.

We also learn about gifts from our parents. My parents had a gift for hospitality. I saw it in our home and at the work place too. My Mom could welcome a new person in our home in a way that seemed to put them right at ease. She knew just how to ask questions about their previous assignment or what their journey to this new installation was like. Somehow she was able to make connections that allowed stories to be shared. Her smile and her ability to listen well made a difference.

Sometimes, I was able to accompany my Dad to his work place. I always liked seeing the place where my Dad worked. It helped me to feel connected to the stories he told at the dinner table. My Dad served as a maintenance officer. I walked with my Dad through hangers as he visited jet engine mechanics and component repair specialists on weekends or holidays. I was always amazed that my Dad would ask how they were tackling a mechanical or avionics problem. His questions allowed the specialist to talk about what they knew as well as what they thought based on their experience. My Dad's inquiries allowed others to share what they were good at. As a leader it was probably tempting to think that he had the answer to the quickest way to solve problems. His questions, however, encouraged the experts to be experts and to share what they knew.

If someone stopped you on the street right now and asked you what your friends say you are good at or what you like to do, how would you answer them? Sometimes in trying to discover our gifts we think that we have to figure it out all on our own. Our parents, our friends, our mentors and members of the Catholic faith community all recognize us and see different gifts in us. They are a resource to pay attention to as we strive to figure it out.

To really discover our gifts though, we need to spend time in prayer with God. Prayer allows us to bring our questions to God. We can ask God what gifts he wants us to use. We can bring to God the things we think we are good at and seek guidance. Our prayer can simply be, 'God show me the way that I might serve others.' In our prayer we also need to spend time quietly listening. We can share with others what we think God is telling us. The leaders of the Church are often tasked with knowing the needs and the gifts of the community. In other words, a good leader in the Church comes to learn the many different gifts of those in that community. When a need arises the leader is able to match those that have the best gifts to serve that particular need. There are many times that we benefited from those that willingly shared their gifts. As members of the Catholic Church we are challenged to move beyond ourselves and share our gifts too.

⊃Reflection Questions
Discovering Giftedness

- What are some things people tell you that you are good at?

- If you could spend your day doing something you really like, what would it be?

- How can you make time to ask God what gifts you have been given and also listen for the answer?

- What are some of the gifts that you see in your parents?

- If there is one gift you wish you had what would it be?

- What are some ways that you have helped your friends in the recent past?

- Can you name a time when someone besides your parents told you that you did something well?

↺Activity
Discovering Giftedness

In the last session you were encouraged to add your faith dimensions to your map. This time you are invited to add to your map the things that you think might be gifts you have discovered along the way.

Giftedness

- In each place that you lived draw a symbol or write a word of something that you were good at or that you liked to do.

- Write down a time where you felt that you were really doing something well and really enjoyed doing it.

- Write down the name of a leader in your community that you respect. What kind of gift does this leader possess?

- When has someone told you that you do something well and you actually agreed with them? What was it?

- If you had to choose what you wanted to do for the rest of your life right now what would you choose?

- What are some ways that you practice the gifts that you think you might have?

⭢Teen and Parent Conversation
Discovering Giftedness

Share your thoughts with one another based on the following questions.

Teen

- What gifts or talents do your friends think you have?

- What are some Catholic *faith skills* that are important to you? (see more about *faith skills* on page 53)

- How have you noticed your parents sharing their gifts with others?

Parent

- What are some gifts that you have and how did you discover them?

- Name a time when you encouraged someone because you saw a gift in them?

- What are some of the gifts that you see in your teenager?

⮫Faith Skills

Faith skills are developed through example and experience. These skills become a part of who we are. They are exhibited in our very being. Faith skills include things like:

- Practicing Empathy
- Reconciling
- Giving Thanks
- Offering Solidarity
- Honoring the Body
- Resolving Conflict[12]

There are three lists of related faith skills on page 116. These lists include religious, moral and emotional skills. Consider which of these skills you already have.

Chapter 2 Notes

[8] *The Catholic Youth Bible*, New Revised Standard Version, revised edition (Winona, MN: Saint Mary's Press, 2005), 6, The Book of Genesis in the Old Testament, Gen. 1:27. Copyright ©2005 by Saint Mary's Press

[9] Map outline found online at http://abcteach.com/Maps/world.htm, accessed on January 2, 2007.

[10] *The Catholic Youth Bible*, 2000, Paul took it upon himself to spread the good news of God's salvation in Jesus to the Gentiles. During three different missionary journeys, he was instrumental in founding new Christian communities...He stayed in touch with these communities through letters, some of which are included as books in the New Testament. Paul's impact

in spreading Christianity was so great that he is sometimes called the second founder of Christianity, 1293.

[11] See *The Catholic Youth Bible*, 1540.

[12] Michael Carotta, EdD, *Nurturing the Spiritual Growth of Your Adolescent*, (Living Our Faith Series, Harcourt Religion Publishers, Orlando, Florida, 2002), 107-130.

3
MOVE:
Faith Connections

In him we move. Military connected families often talk about being moved from place to place. Sometimes they are asked if they like it or not. But, there is more to moving than the permanent change of stations. There is the reality of friends moving in and out of our lives each year. There is the movement of change in family life as we prepare for and experience deployments. There is also the movement of self when one strives so hard to fit in that they erase themselves and their needs. A faith-filled life helps us to deal with these many transitions when we recognize that the presence of God moves within us too. These reflections guide us in reflecting upon how moving affects us.

Saying Goodbye: Reconciliation

One of the hardest things to do as a military connected youth is to figure out how to say goodbye well. We have friends that move in and out of our lives every year. You would think that we would be good at it based on experience alone. Often, when we hear of a friend's departure date we either try to spend as much time as possible with that friend or figure out a way that we can be angry with them so that the actual departure does not hurt so much. Of course, when our family moves we experience total loss. It seems that everything we were connected to will be gone: our home, our friends, our school, a culture we grew accustomed to and role models that we grew to admire.

The military culture has developed a simple way of saying goodbye and welcoming the newcomer with a gathering for those on active duty often referred to as a 'hail and farewell.' At many installations military units gather to pay tribute to those that will be moving on and to welcome those that recently arrived. This monthly ritual allows a designated time for those in uniform to acknowledge change, to say a word of thanks or a word of welcome.

Unfortunately, there is no such ritual for military connected youth or families. Families or friends have to come up with their own way of saying goodbye. For military connected youth this can be a challenge since throughout each year we experience friends depart or we have to deal with departing ourselves. With these multiple departures it can be tempting to just walk away and never say farewell. On the surface it seems easier. Once we learn that our family will be moving to a new assignment we have to watch ourselves to make sure that we don't slowly disengage from the relationships that have mattered to us.

Goodbye seems like such a final word. Many of us hope that we might cross paths again but we are never really sure if we will. Sometimes we leave without ever resolving an argument or acknowledging that we hurt someone. Departing without reconciling seems as though it will be a quick solution. With each move it becomes easier to just pack up and go without ever really saying goodbye. This is where extra baggage comes into play. We carry with us all of the friendships and relationships that we have had wherever we go. If we choose not to reconcile or give thanks for the time that was spent together than our baggage becomes heavier. Later in life we will have what is referred to as 'unresolved grief.' Loss is meant to be mourned. It is difficult and it requires a letting go. If we choose to avoid it the unresolved grief will creep up at a later time and it can become a heavy load to carry.

In the Catholic faith we celebrate the sacrament of reconciliation. We prepare for this sacrament through an examination of conscience. That means that we look back on our life and examine the times that we have hurt others, hurt God, or even hurt ourselves. Reconciliation is a sacrament that allows us to recognize our sins and admit the times that we have broken the relationships that matter to us. Through this sacrament we receive the forgiveness of God and we hope to move forward to treat all of our relationships with a deeper respect.

The life of Jesus shows us how to say goodbye well. In his public ministry, Jesus and the disciples traveled to many places. An encounter with Jesus was a deeply personal and profound experience. Some of the encounters were brief one-on-one experiences. Some were collective experiences among crowds on a hillside. Some of the experiences with Christ involved healings and miracles and some involved welcoming Jesus for a meal around the table. Jesus knew how to give gratitude to God for the time he spent with others no matter how brief the encounter may have been. Through a look, a touch, or even a word, Jesus was able to let the other know that they were a gift in his life. This model provides a way for us to begin to think about how we may recognize one another as a gift. We accept that gift when we say 'thank you.' Our life of transitions challenges us to give thanks each time we encounter a departure.

↪Reflection Questions
Saying Goodbye

- When was the last time you said goodbye to a good friend?

- How were you able to let that friend know that they mattered to you?

- Have you ever just walked away from a friendship without acknowledging it?

- What are some practical ways that you can reconcile with others?

- If you could re-live a bad departure what would you do differently?

- What are some ways that others have said goodbye to you?

- How can your family help you when you have to deal with another friend leaving?

⊃Journal
Saying Goodbye

Graduating with Friends

Jon (not the person's actual name) was a high school senior growing up in a military connected family. He liked hanging out with friends and trying new things. A month before Jon was going to graduate he found out that his family would move from an overseas assignment back to the United States since his Dad had received orders for a new assignment. Jon had been preparing for the past few months to graduate with his friends. This new assignment meant that he would depart two weeks before the graduation ceremony and he would miss all of the celebrations. Jon knew his family would be moving sometime over the summer but the orders came early and now they would have to go sooner. Later that week the high school principal handed Jon his diploma in her office. There was no public recognition of his accomplishment, no rejoicing, no pictures with family and friends - there was no pomp and circumstance.

A community of friends gathered with Jon the night before he was to fly back to the United States. They set up a mock graduation with a makeshift cap and gown, and a rolled up scroll of paper. The ceremony even included slightly off-key humming of the traditional graduation music. While this small ritual offered a way to reach out to Jon a more important experience unfolded.

That evening Jon's friends shared with him one thing about him that made a difference in their lives or the lives of others in the community. After each person shared Jon was invited to share one thing he remembered about everyone present. The sharing helped to develop the skills of hospitality and gratitude by enabling all of them to say goodbye well. These young people experienced the joy and sorrow of sending someone forth with the knowledge that their presence impacted the lives of others. They learned how to show gratitude for the gift of time that was shared. They learned an appropriate way to say thank you. This experience was at times hard since it is not easy to say goodbye. On the other hand, it also brought about smiles and laughter as memories were shared.

Saying goodbye well in this context did not require a six week program of learned behaviors. Instead a need was met through the expression of gratitude. It was a moment of sending forth that helped everyone present to unpack their experiences and recognize the gift of time. It recognized the profound impact of human worth by sharing the ways that a person's life impacted others for the good. In many ways, an experience like this is similar to the many people Jesus met during his years of ministry. On the road, out in the world, Jesus encountered people longing to live a good life. "Master, what must I do to gain eternal life?" Jesus shared with them a way to follow, a way to be a disciple. The people Jesus encountered where lifted up and encouraged. Their sins were forgiven and they were blessed with a sense to share these gifts with others.

- What strikes you about Jon's story?

- What would it be like if you were Jon in this story?

- What are some creative ways that you could acknowledge friends that are departing?

- What are some of the memorable departures you have experienced?

➲Teen and Parent Conversation
Saying Goodbye

Share your thoughts with one another based on the following questions.

Teen

- What is your first reaction when you learn that your family has to move to a new assignment?

- What are some ways that you have helped your family when all of you were packing up and saying goodbye?

- If you could thank your parent for one thing they do to help you through the many transitions you deal with what would it be?

Parent

- What about moving or seeing friends move is difficult for you?

- Are there times that you have experienced a departure without reconciliation? What did that feel like then and what does it feel like now?

- If you could thank your teenager for one thing they do to help your family with the many transitions they deal with what would it be?

⊃Examination of Conscience

The Catholic tradition has a preparation for the Sacrament of Reconciliation known as an examination of conscience. Through prayer we look back and examine the ways we have broken relationships or hurt others with our words, our actions, or even our avoidance. This page includes a list to take to prayer. It can be used by military connected youth and parents to pray with several months prior to leaving their current assignment. It is by no means an exhaustive list but it provides a series of questions that demand our attention so that we may reconcile with God and with those that God has put in our life.

- When was the last time I prayed?

- Is prayer a consistent practice in my daily life?

- Have I ignored God?

- Have I turned away from what God wants for me?

- Have I failed to serve others?

- Have I ignored the newcomer on my installation?

- Have I avoided challenges by relying on artificial escapes like alcohol, drugs, or sex?

- Have I tried to "fit in" by becoming somebody that I am not?

- Have I said goodbye to those departing and thanked them for the gifts they shared?

- Have I attempted to reconcile with those I have argued with or fought with?

- Have I been willing to forgive others?

- Have I made time to reflect and pray?

- Have I listened to my parents?

- Have I helped out at home during times of transition, such as moving, deployments, and trainings?

- Have I allowed others to welcome me when I am the newcomer?

- Have I lived my Catholic faith so that others recognize that it makes a difference in my life?

- Have I recognized the presence of Christ in people, places and simple things?

- Have I really tried to discover the gifts that God has given me?

God Moves Me:
Entering With God's Grace

There is a deeper part to saying goodbye that many of us forget when we move. Travel can be so quick these days that before we know it we are in our new location and we haven't fully mourned the loss of what we have left behind. This creates awkward moments where we carry our longing for what was familiar into unfamiliar territory. Sometimes, we just need someone to listen to us articulate the things and the people that we miss. We unpack our mourning by finding ways to release and let go.

Our parents are going through the same process when we move but, they also have to figure out where we will live, how to set up a new house, what their new job requirements will be along with all of the other details that are required to process into a new assignment. Parents can sometimes try to change the focus of their teenagers by encouraging them to see the good things about their new location. They might even suggest that this is what being in a military connected family is all about so get use to it. In reality, letting go takes time and is hard to do when you are a stranger in a new place.

Finding your way in a new location is more than just figuring out directions and schedules. We begin to develop new relationships too. Some of us are good at making new friends right away. Others take more time to meet new people. Each one of us knows what it is like to walk into a new school without knowing anyone there. To be alone in a crowd can be one of the most daunting experiences of transition.

Military connected youth that move in and out of different cultures develop a broader view of the world. They hear the news with a vested interest regarding stories about the places they have been. These positive outer experiences can also lead to a desire to fit in wherever we move. Our ability to quickly learn new cultures or ways of being becomes a survival skill that we develop along the way. One of the dangers of this acquired skill is that we change our very self to fit it. Military connected youth have a keen sense of observation. We have learned to survive by quickly assessing what is happening around us and adapting to fit in. Just as our lives change and adapt during deployments we notice that same thing happens when we move to a new assignment too. We might quickly identify a group that we want to be a part of and then figure out how to fit in so that we will be accepted. We can, almost like a chameleon, change our way of being so that we will no longer feel like a stranger even though we are still mourning what we have left behind.

Staying connected to our sustaining relationships, with faith and family, we remember that no matter where we go or what we experience we are never really alone. God moves us and moves within us. By that I mean that God guides us in these new locations to grow and to share our gifts with others. Each installation comes with unique experiences that provide life-giving encounters and challenges that are a part of daily living. In prayer people often say that they are moved by God. It may be a spiritual or emotional feeling of being touched by the creator. In our prayer, God moves us by reminding us that in him we live and move and have our being, (see Acts of the Apostles 17:28). God also listens to us with a comforting and guiding hand as we mourn our losses and wonder how we will make it in this new place.

Our immediate family, like God, knows our life story. These important relationships in our lives recognize when we are adapting too much and are no longer truly ourselves. They remind us that we fit in the most just by being the person that God created us to be. Our family can listen, provide comfort, and understand what it really means to deal with so many losses. They have experienced the same things, sometimes in different ways but they know what it means to experience loss too. A brief look at your life map can remind you of the many influences in your life that have shaped you and guided you along the way. In the center of all of those experiences remains the presence of your family and your faith. When we continually turn to these constants in our lives we recognize them as gifts that sustain us and we can truly enter a new community with God's grace.

↻Reflection Questions
God Moves Me

- In your most recent move what did you leave behind that you miss the most?

- How long did it take you to feel like you were part of your new community?

- What sort of changes have you made to fit into a new place?

- When you really need someone to just listen who can you turn to?

- What are some ways that you have recognized God moving you?

- How do you recognize God as a part of your life story?

- What do your parents do well to help you adjust to your new location?

↺Journal
God Moves Me

> There was no funeral.
> No flowers.
> No ceremony.
> No one had died.
> No weeping or wailing.
> Just in my heart.
> *I can't...*
> But I did anyway,
> and nobody knew I couldn't.
> *I don't want to...*
> But nobody else said they didn't.
> So I put down my panic
> and picked up my luggage
> and got on the plane.
> There was no funeral.[13]
> ~"Mock Funeral"
> By Alex Graham James

Find a quite space and spend some time writing your thoughts and experiences in a journal. You might choose to write a letter to God about the obvious and the hidden losses from your last move (see page 71 for a list). What was it like for you to say goodbye and mourn the loss of friends and familiar places the last time you moved. Think of specific things that you miss being a part of. After writing take some time to pray and ask God what it is that you are being moved towards now that you are in your new home.

➲Losses
God Moves Me

Obvious losses include:
A loss of friends
A loss of a home that you were comfortable in
A loss of a school system that you understood
A loss of places where you hung out
A loss of activities that you could only do in your
previous location
What are other obvious losses?

Hidden losses include:
A loss of the world as you knew it
A loss of status
A loss of lifestyle
A loss of possessions (what are some of the things
that you physically left behind?)
A loss of relationships
A loss of role model(s)
A loss of identity in a system you were familiar with
A loss of the past that wasn't (things that you
missed that can't be replaced, like a parent
deployed during your birthday or being away
from extended family during the holidays)
A loss of the past that was (a history that you left
behind), see footnote 13 for a reference that goes
into more detail on hidden losses and unresolved
grief due to the transition of moving.
What are other hidden losses that you would add to
this list?

⟳Teen and Parent Conversation
God Moves Me

Share your thoughts with one another based on the following questions.

Teen

- What is the hardest thing about being a stranger in a new assignment?

- How can you find time or space to mourn the loss of and pray about the things you miss?

- How does your parent offer comfort during these times of transition?

Parent

- How do you feel like a stranger in a new assignment?

- What do you do to mourn the loss of the people or things you miss?

- How does your faith help you deal with a life of transitions?

Moving in Place:
The Challenge of Deployments

Deployments have had a huge impact on military connected families in past the few years. Many resources have been produced to assist young children with the realities of these long separations. There is currently a very limited amount of resources available for adolescents that have a parent deployed. Many of the resources that are available include checklists of things to do or not to do. In the introduction of this resource I acknowledged that my own personal experience with deployments is limited. I know a little bit about it from memories shared when I was a young child and my dad was on a one year remote assignment in Thailand. More recently I learned about the effects of deployment from listening to the experiences of teenagers in military connected families today. Their experiences are vivid, powerful and challenging.

In 2003, when the United States military began sending troops to Afghanistan and Iraq, I was serving as the Catholic youth ministry leader at the U.S. Army Post Chapel in Heidelberg, Germany. One of the most powerful stories of that time was a family that was preparing to say goodbye to their dad. He was going to be away for at least six months but they weren't sure if that time would be extended or not. Danielle, (not the person's actual name) who was part of a small Catholic peer leader group, shared that even though it would be hard for her family to have their dad away they had prepared as much as they could. They were now just waiting to find out when he would actually depart. Finally, the day came when Danielle's dad told the family that he would be shipping out the next day. That night they had a family dinner, they re-checked lists they had made going over who would be responsible for what, and they prayed together asking God to guide each member of the family through this new stage of family life. The next morning they all got up and said their goodbyes which were difficult and filled with lots of tears and hugs. Danielle's mom drove her dad to his unit and all of the kids made their way to the bus stop to continue with the normal routine of their daily lives. That night each family member made their way back home including Danielle's dad. His plane had not taken off that day so all of the unit members were sent back home. That night was a repeat of the night before and the next morning the family went through the goodbye process of tears and hugs again. That night they all came home and as they were eating dinner their dad walked through the door again. This happened four nights in a row. The goodbyes were emotionally draining. Each family member had difficulty staying focused at school or even listening to their friends. On the fourth day, Danielle's dad and his unit finally boarded their plane and began their journey to the Persian Gulf.

During that week Danielle shared that it was really difficult for her to say goodbye to her dad each day of the week. She was torn because although she was grateful to have another day with her dad, she hated waking up the next morning to go through the hugs and tears of departure again. It was emotionally draining on every family member.

Danielle said that she sometimes wished her dad would just go to a hotel so they wouldn't have to deal with the suffering of saying goodbye again. Danielle wasn't looking for an answer to these challenging days, she wasn't even looking to find out if her feelings were right or wrong. What Danielle needed the most was to share her experience with friends and mentors that would listen well.

Deployments bring about a wide variety of new lived experiences that provide challenges, accomplishments and suffering. The challenges are numerous because the military connected family is stretched to be family while they are apart. The accomplishments come in discovering that through a lot of effort each family member can pitch in and make a difference. Teenagers, especially those with younger siblings, are often relied on to do quite a bit to maintain some sense of normalcy in the house. There is also the reality of suffering. It hurts to miss the one you love. It is hard to watch the parent at home struggle. Not knowing exactly where your deployed parent is on a particular day or what type of mission they are involved with increases tension and stress as the unknowns seem to just pile one on top of the other.

Deployments offer a time for a new type of pilgrimage because each family member is being moved into a new way of living. Any kind of movement presents change. We have experienced changes many times in our own moves from place to place. To be on pilgrimage in your own home seems strange because in many ways you are moving in place. The place that was once familiar is now different due to the loss of the presence of your deployed parent. A deployed pilgrimage presents an opportunity for reconnecting with the important relationships in your life. Those relationships include your family and your prayer life with Christ. When we are suffering the most these are the relationships that we can turn to with the reminder that we are not alone. You may think that your parent at home doesn't understand what you are going through. You have to remind yourself that they are also dealing with the stress of trying to keep it together. They may not totally understand where you are coming from but, you need to take time to share your challenges and frustrations. You also need to attempt to listen to what some of your parents frustrations are. A pilgrimage of any sort stretches us beyond what we think are our limits. A deployed pilgrimage helps us to see beyond ourselves, to consider the needs of others and to grow in our commitment to rely God and those that love us.

Prayer is a conversation with God that changes and moves us. When we make time to pray and connect with God we open our hearts and our minds to the one who loves us. Christ moves throughout our lives and knows what is happening to us. We feel the presence of Christ in the touch of friend who really hears us. As we receive the body of Christ in the Eucharist we experience that our true home is found in being a child of God. We see Christ in the people and places around us that help us to understand that God is moving throughout the world all the time. This doesn't mean that there isn't suffering. Difficult things happen but God's presence surrounds us. When we feel there is too much change, or the experience of deployment is too hard we need to open our eyes to see Christ moving us and moving people into our lives as we continue our pilgrimage.

⟳Reflection Questions
Moving in Place

- What has changed in my life as a result of deployments?

- When have you experienced spiritual growth while moving in place? In other words, how have you noticed God's presence as the challenges of deployments have stretched you?

- What are some of the new life skills that you are developing as a result of your parent being deployed? What are some of the new things that you have learned to do in their absence?

- How is God present in the lives of those who are deployed?

- How is God present in the lives of the people of Iraq and Afghanistan?

- What sort of changes has my deployed parent had to deal with?

- How does the deployed pilgrimage stretch you?

➲Journal
Moving in Place

Mike Vandesteeg was a teenager when his dad was deployed to the first Gulf War in 1990. His mother Carol, who wrote a book for families about dealing with deployment, asked Mike to write down his thoughts on what helped him get through his dad's deployment. Read the five things Mike wrote and then spend some time writing in your journal about the five things that help you get through the time when a parent is deployed. If your parent hasn't deployed yet you might write the five things that are helping you deal with the possibility of your parent being deployed.

These five things helped me get through Dad's Desert Shield/Desert Storm deployment:

1. Faith: Shaky as it may have been, faith gave me an indescribable peace. That may not mean that everything made sense, just that there was comfort in knowing that things were out of my hands. I had no control over it, and that was OK.

2. Letters, phone calls, e-mail, care packages, etc. from home and from the deployed parent. That helps immensely, because even if a kid won't admit it, it helps him feel connected across the miles. I've never been the best

communicator, but it is/was good to hear from my parents, whether I said that or not.

3. Community of friends and family. Both groups are important. Family, because they are involved as they are also related to the deployed family member. Friends, because they helped me to stay busy. Going to someone's house for dinner or out to a movie really helped. As a subset of this, I thought it was invaluable to have two or three close friends who I could confide in, sort of spill my guts as needed, and have access to them whenever I needed them.

4. Activity: studying, reading, sports, etc. I probably spent most of my time with friends or playing sports when dad was deployed, more than I did at any other time. Those were my two main release mechanisms.

5. Connecting with other kids whose parents are in the military, whether they were deployed or not. It was always good to meet someone like that because they understood better than anyone else what I was going through.

Looking back on the many years that have passed since that time, I think I have learned much. My faith in God is much stronger (to say the least) than it was at that time. Although I may not have been very close to God at that time, in hindsight I can see that he was close to me even though I didn't realize it. [14]

What strikes you about Mike's list? Write a list, in your own words, of things that would help you when your parent deploys or things that did help you when your parent was deployed.

↰Teen and Parent Conversation
Moving In Place

Share your thoughts with one another based on the following questions.

Teen

- What is a real life story about deployment that you have heard about or experienced?

- What does your parent at home do that makes the challenge of deployment a little bit easier?

- What are the challenges, accomplishments and sufferings that you have experienced during a deployment?

Parent

- What is it like for you to remain at home with many of the responsibilities?

- How do you make time for prayer during the deployment cycle?

- What are the challenges, accomplishments and sufferings that you have experienced during a deployment?

Moving with Faith: Recognizing Catholicism around the World

Growing up Catholic in a military connected family is a great gift. I have already mentioned some of the experiences of feeling welcomed as we move in and out of different Catholic faith communities. Whether we go to church at the installation chapel or at the local parish off base we are blessed with recognizing something that is familiar. The Catholic Mass is a ritual that welcomes us. At Mass the Liturgy of the Word and the Liturgy of the Eucharist re-members and re-connects us with Jesus Christ along with the community of faith that sustains us.

No matter where we move in the world we travel with our Catholic faith. If we are assigned overseas we can participate in Mass in a foreign language and pretty well understand exactly what is happening. We may not be able to translate the homily but we certainly are familiar with the parts of the mass because they are similar all around the world. From the beginning of mass with the opening song and the procession of the cross down the main aisle to the final blessing and the sign of the cross, we recognize that we are at home in unfamiliar places.

We bring our Catholic identity with us wherever we travel. Being Catholic is a part of who we are. The traditions of Catholicism, the teachings of the church and the Catholic bible all shape our path of life. If prayer is a part of our daily lives then it can be easier for us to recognize this gift. If, however, we only pray during times of need or trouble then we may find that it takes us some time to recognize the great gift for connection that we have.

We recognize important faith connections when we pray by ourselves as well as in community. Catholics highly value both of these. As Catholics we practice prayer. That practice might stretch us to become comfortable with silence or listening. Discovering ways that we pray well can be its own sort of pilgrimage since there are so many different styles of prayer. Whether we connect through music, through reading the bible, through journaling, through finding time alone to walk with God or by making space to acknowledge God somehow each day, we are participating in a life-giving relationship that grows and changes and helps us deal with changes too.

Catholics have customs, traditions and seasons that allow military connected families to easily carry family and faith traditions with them wherever they move.

- The season of Advent, when we pray and wait for the birth of Christ
- The season of Christmas, when we rejoice in the awareness of the presence of Christ
- The season of Lent, when we designate times for fasting and letting go
- The celebration of Holy Week, the holiest time of the year when we remember Christ's call to serve one another just as he did through washing feet, we also recall the suffering of Jesus, his death on the cross, and Jesus rising again (resurrection)

- The season of Easter, when we celebrate joy that reminds us of hope in life everlasting
- The celebration of Ordinary time, when we recall that our Catholic identity is a part of our daily living
- The Holy Days of Obligation, when we make time to remember special events[15]

These liturgical seasons and celebrations occur at specific times throughout the liturgical year, every year no matter where we move.

The themes of these liturgical celebrations and remembrances have something to say to those of us living a life on the move. They remind us to connect in faith through the struggles and joys that we experience such as:

- Seeking the light of Christ in our world that many times feels or appears dark, (Advent)
- Rejoicing when someone welcomes us or we welcome a stranger, (Christmas)
- Letting go of the people, places, and things we have become familiar with (Lent)
- Recognizing that there are times of suffering and grieving when our family moves but also realizing that new life awaits us that will bring us hope (Holy Week)
- Seeing first hand that people around the world recognize and celebrate the joy of Jesus Christ by living as Easter people (Easter Joy)
- Struggling with daily decisions, longing for what we don't have and yet recognizing that Christ gives us all that we need for daily living (Ordinary Time)

- Connecting with relationships, leaders, mentors and those that who practice what it means to identify themselves as Catholic (Holy Days of Obligation)

There are many ways that we are rooted in faith even though we keep getting transplanted. It is exciting to be Catholic in the world because there are so many ways to identify with a community of faith that knows where we are coming from and where we are heading.

⟳Reflection Questions
Moving with Faith

- If you had to tell someone what it means to be Catholic what would you say?

- What is something about the Catholic faith that is familiar to you?

- What are some things about being Catholic that you really like?

- What are some things about being Catholic that leave you with questions?

- What is your favorite Catholic season, feast day or holy day?

- How does your family celebrate being Catholic?

- When have you been at Mass in a new location and yet recognized something familiar?

↪Journal
Moving with Faith

Pico Iyer grew up shuttling between England and California, the son of Indian immigrant parents. His writings highlight that the benefits of travel contribute to a multinational soul on a multinational globe which allows one to feel at home everywhere in the world. This lifestyle can also produce a sense of dispassion because we find that we are not deeply connected to any particular place at all. Pico writes:

Airports are among the only sites in public life where emotions are hugely sanctioned, in block capitals. We see people weep, shout, kiss in airports; we see them at the furthest edges of excitement and exhaustion. Airports are privileged spaces where we can see the primal states writ large-fear, recognition, hope. But there are some of us, perhaps, sitting at the Departure Gate, boarding passes in hand, watching the destinations ticking over, who feel neither the pain of separation nor the exultation of wonder; who alight with the same emotions with which embarked; who go down to the baggage carousel and watch our lives circling, circling, circling, waiting to be claimed.[16]

In your Journal spend some time writing about your thoughts to Pico's quote. Can you identify with the idea of your life, circling like baggage, waiting to be claimed? How can you claim your life and live it to the full? Who can help you do that? How does the Catholic faith give you something to be passionate about and to live for?

➲Teen and Parent Conversation
Moving With Faith

Teen

- What is important to you about being Catholic?

- How does the Catholic faith help you deal with transitions and moving?

- What are some of the ways that you currently practice prayer?

Parent

- What is it about being Catholic that helps you connect with your past?

- Where can you learn more about the holy days of obligation?

- What are some of the ways that you currently practice prayer?

Chapter 3 Notes

[13] Unpublished poem by Alex Graham James found in the book by David C. Pollack and Ruth E. Van Reken, *Third Culture Kids: The Experience of Growing Up Among Worlds*, (Nicholas Brealey Publishing, Boston, Massachusetts, 2001)165. This poem begins Chapter 11, Unresolved Grief. See this chapter for more detail about the hidden losses that young people who move experience. These include loss of their world, loss of status, loss of lifestyle, loss of possessions, loss of relationships, loss of role models, loss of system identity, loss of the past that wasn't and loss of the past that was.

[14] Carol Vandesteeg, *When Duty Calls: A Handbook for Families Facing Military Separation*, (Life Journey, Colorado Springs, CO, 2005), 132-133.

[15] In the United States of America we celebrate six holy days of obligation. These include: Christmas, Ascension, Mary, Mother of God, Immaculate Conception, Assumption, and All Saints. See Rev. Peter Klein, *The Catholic Source Book* (Third Edition, Brown-ROA, Orlando, Florida, 2000), 342.

[16] Faith Eidse and Nina Sichel, Editors, *Unrooted Childhoods: Memoirs of Growing Up Global*, (Intercultural Press, Yarmouth, Maine), 2004, 16-17.

4
BEING:
Living Our Catholic Faith

In him we have our being. Military connected families can fall into the trap of living a segmented life. This means that we have the potential to put boundaries on our experiences in each location. We can also bracket the relationships that we develop. Life, in other words, can be viewed as a dispassionate collection of experiences that do not connect with one another. Being is a state of living and it is a vital part of who we are. Being in God is a life giving way of living that enables us to connect our experiences and grow in the relationships that matter. Every human being has the potential to respond to God and make a difference by serving others. Living our Catholic faith takes seriously what it means to be a believer in the world today. When we view our 'life on the move' as a pilgrimage, then we take time to notice and reflect. The final four reflections are designed to help us unpack the gifts we have picked up as a pilgrim on this journey of faith which help us to identify our very being.

Recognizing the Presence of Christ: The Simple Things

Young people that grow up among different cultures face two obvious states of being that are identified as rootlessness and restlessness.[17] Living in multiple cultures and experiencing different ways of living often translates into never quite having full ownership of our own sense of being. A large tree is rooted in one place. Those roots grow and travel underground seeking nourishment from the earth where it is planted. A rooted tree also receives nourishment from the sun and rain above the ground. Our life tree has many of the same aspects except for being rooted in one location. Our tree is mobile and it reaches out, like branches towards the sky, seeking growth from what it encounters, above the ground, wherever it may be at that time. When we move we have to be creative to seek out nourishment in new environments. At the same time we possess roots within us that ground our experiences as we are repeatedly transplanted. Our restlessness, on the other hand, dwells in our desire to experience being rooted in one place. It is, in a sense, a longing for what our being is not. Restlessness causes us to easily become dissatisfied with the present situation no matter where we are.

Rootlessness is as basic as the physical reality that we don't have a place to call home. We are not planted anywhere. When we sense that no one will understand where we are coming from, we avoid talking about our lived experiences. We can feel alone in a new community because others, especially those that are physically rooted, cannot relate to our life of multiple cultures. We can become expert *observers* noticing what is different in our new environment. Often we notice from afar, as though we are reporting on what is happening rather than being intertwined among the experiences of that new culture. Rootlessness, at its worst, keeps us from making life giving connections or engaging with others to share the story of our pilgrimage.

Restlessness is found in both our past and present situations. No matter where we are we sense that it is never enough, something always seems to be lacking. It is found in the struggle of moving to a new place while missing or wanting what we had before. Restlessness dwells in us wherever we live, when we desire a history that is not a part of who we are. Sometimes, moving every few years means that we never wholeheartedly jump into our new environment. Our restlessness causes a dissatisfaction that finds us surfing cultures. We can easily skim across the top of our cultural experiences without living deeply the experiences that are directly in front of us. This is similar to surfing on the internet which can result in never locating our intended destination. Surfing culture, like surfing the internet, can be a wandering experience that keeps us living on the surface. In a new culture it may appear that we are fully present and finding our way but in reality we are just going through the motions and following whatever path presents itself at the time. Our restlessness causes us to believe that there is a place, somewhere, anywhere, which will provide all that we are looking for. Restlessness is our longing to be rooted with the hope that our identity will be better understood.

The Christian life is focused on the simple things. A life well lived is rooted in gospel values rather than things or places that we hold onto. As Christians we live between the already and the not yet. Believers have a sense of the Kingdom of God because they recognize the presence of Christ. At the same time they realize that that kingdom has not yet been fully realized. There is hope in the promise of what is to come, a time when the Kingdom of God will indeed be fully realized.

In some ways, we could say that Christians live daily with the experiences of rootlessness and restlessness. We strive to live a good life but we make mistakes along the way. We long for the day when all will get along as we hear and experience the many ways that violence tears people apart. We want to find a home in Christ but we worry about having enough money so that we can take care of our own needs without relying on the help of others. We hope in the reality of everlasting life in heaven but our daily existence finds us ignoring others or focusing on our own needs at the expense of the poor.

St. Augustine, one of the famous Church fathers, struggled between living for himself and living the way that God called him into being. His writings recount his life story and tell about how he came to grapple with problems of the world while growing to understand the will of God. St. Augustine was the first Christian to regard human experience – notably his own life story – as the first starting point for reflecting on God.[18] St. Augustine's search led him to realize that restlessness is part of the human condition. In his famous book, *Confessions*, he wrote in the first chapter:

> You stir man to take pleasure in praising you, because you have made us for yourself, and our heart is restless until it rests in you.[19]

Our soul is designed to be rooted in faith. As we embrace hope we become more capable of dealing with restlessness. Recognizing the presence of Christ calls us to be in relationship. Through individual and communal prayer, through serving those in need with our gifts and through changing our focus we notice Christ present in our lives and in our world.

Christ's presence is alive in the simplicity of creation, like a small flower or a beautiful day. Christ's presence is recognized in the face of everyone we pass by. Christ's presence is realized in the celebration of the Eucharist when the real presence of Christ becomes one with our very being. Christ is recognized in the simple things. If we truly believe that our hearts rest in Christ than we have a place where we belong and we have a place to bring uneasiness. There is hope, in the daily recognition of the simple things, that our faith in Christ provides the very roots of our being.

⮌Reflection Questions
Recognizing the Presence of Christ

- How have you felt rootlessness in your life?

- How have you experienced restlessness in your life?

- What is one way that you could describe your sense of being right now?

- Name a time when you surfed through a place or experience?

- How does your Catholic faith help you live more deeply?

- What are simple things that help you recognize the presence of Christ?

- Where did you recognize Christ this week?

➲Experience
Recognizing the Presence of Christ

Mini pilgrimage

Spend half-a-day with your parent noticing the presence of Christ.

- Find a park, a forest or some place surrounded by nature where you can both walk. Spend thirty minutes to an hour searching for something in nature that reminds you of Christ. Decide if you are going to walk together or journey out on your own. Once you have found your object spend some time praying. Let God know how you notice Christ's presence. Listen to what God is sharing with you. *Share with one another why you picked what you did and how it draws you to see Christ.*

- Visit the Blessed Sacrament Chapel on your military installation or visit a Catholic church in your community. Together spend twenty to thirty minutes praying quietly to God. *Share one or two things in the chapel that remind you of the presence of Christ. Share a memory of Church when you really felt the presence of Christ.*

- Visit a shopping mall, a bus station or an airport. Find a bench to sit on and spend twenty to thirty minutes just watching people go by. *Share in what or whom you recognized the presence of Christ during that time.*

- Visit a place to eat that you might normally go to. Share a snack or a meal. *In this time of being served where do you recognize Christ?*

- At the end of the mini pilgrimage pray the *Our Father* together and in your own words thank God for the gift of Christ's presence in our world today.

This mini pilgrimage carves out time from your normal schedule to quietly look for the presence of Christ in the real world. Try not to let the worries and concerns of daily living creep into this experience. This is not a time to run errands between experiences. It is designed to be a time dedicated for parent and teen to go out into the world and seek Christ together.

⟳Teen and Parent Conversation
Recognizing the Presence of Christ

Share your thoughts with one another based on the following questions.

Teen

- Where are you feeling restlessness at this point in your life?

- How does the Catholic faith help you find roots in your soul?

- Where are some the places that you are recognizing Christ?

Parent

- How do you cope with the reality of restlessness?

- Why can it be difficult to believe that God will provide?

- Where are some of the places that you are recognizing Christ?

Praying Our Experiences:
Moving Forward, Reflecting Back

One of my good friends in high school liked to go deer hunting with his dad. Every Monday, during hunting season, I received a play-by-play reenactment of his entire weekend sitting atop a deer blind, waiting in silence. When I first began listening to these stories I would roll my eyes and wonder when that day's tale would finally end. I was not a hunter or even someone who spent time camping. As the weeks went by though I became intrigued with how much my friend experienced while waiting. I began to look forward to his Monday morning stories because I became amazed at how much he noticed in silence. Through his descriptions I was able to see the landscape, the trees and the bushes that blocked his view. I learned about young fawns and mature bucks that were able to fool the hunter and escape on a moment's notice. I grew to appreciate that his experiences were not marked by time regulated on a clock. My friend loved being out there, soaking it all in.

Prayer offers us the opportunity to slow down, to be silent and to soak it all in. When we pray we reflect on our life experiences, our emotions and our faith. We also pray for the needs of the church, the community, and the world. Prayer is the expression of our relationship with God. In prayer we recognize God who has given us the gift of life, the gift to question, and the gift to give thanks. When we make time to reflect on our lives through prayer we unpack the variety of experiences we have collected. Prayer allows us to experience the sacred.

Life on the go can become a routine of moving forward. We move, unpack, attempt to settle in, exist or survive through the current assignment, learn about the next assignment, pack up and move to the new location only to repeat the same cycle. A life of faith can become a routine of moving forward too. Our prayer life can be seen as a collection of gatherings, from Sunday to Sunday, without any connection or reflection. Moving forward is a natural mode for the mobile life. Finding a way to reflect back is a skill that helps us to practice unpacking the experiences collected along the way. In prayer we begin to recognize the gift of God's relationship throughout our lives.

A life of moving forward is more than a collection of addresses, people and experiences. In reflecting back, the people and places in our lives can become important touchstones that help us to frame and better understand our lived experience. We live, and grow and change with each new experience. In prayer we make the time to remember, and sometimes see in new ways, how those experiences have shaped us. We begin to uncover the ways that God has been moving us too.

Young people growing up among different cultures have many of the same basic needs as young people rooted in one culture. These include the need for strong relationships; a sense of belonging, of being nurtured and cared for, of internal unity, of significance; and a feeling of knowing ourselves and being known by others. Every human also has the need to express in one way or another the emotional, creative, intellectual, volitional, and spiritual aspects of his or her being.[20]

When we pray we discover. What we discover is meant to be shared with others. The communal part of our discernment is found in the relationships that we trust enough to share what is really going on in our lives. It is in the small group[21] that we are able to tell our story, share our needs and explore the ways in which we are responding to God. Our greatest sense of belonging can be identified in our pilgrim faith. As a Catholic pilgrim we live our developing faith into our whole being. Our true identity, no matter where we are, becomes our understanding of the person that God created us to be which we discover in prayer.

Through our reflection and prayer we begin to map out our experiences over time, in the light of faith. When we reflect back we recognize God's presence in our daily life. We become open to the possibilities of God's grace when we dream about what could be. Dreams that find us reconciling with others or reaching out to lend a hand. Finally, prayer calls for a response. There is a give and take in this relationship. It is in prayer that we are moved to act. The movement may be slow or it may result in a quick turn around. As pilgrims of faith we acknowledge that our prayer moves us into being.

⮑Reflection Questions
Praying Our Experiences

- When do you most feel like you are only moving forward?

- How do you listen to God?

- Where or when do you most experience the presence of God?

- What are you dreaming about these days?

- How do you think you are being called to act or respond to God?

- Who makes up the small group of relationships that you can truly share with?

- Can you identify with belonging as a Catholic pilgrim?

⊃Experience
Praying Our Experiences

Individual and communal reflection

With a parent or a couple of close friends spend some time reflecting on the phrases listed below. You might pray in silence, or chose to write down a few thoughts or journal about one or two of the phrases that really speak to you. After at least a half hour of silence, share what your responses were as you prayed and reflected upon these phrases.

- Where are you from...?

- How have you belonged and yet belonged nowhere...?

- What do you want to do with the rest of your life...?

- How do you seek permanence in frequent transition...?

- When do most focus on moving forward and not looking back...?

- What are some ways that you can adapt well...?

- What are some ways that you are able to find silence...?

- How is home a state of mind...?

- How can you be at home in Christ...?

- When are you able to really listen to God...?

- When did you last tell your story...?

- What dreams are you dreaming...?

- How do you express your feelings...?

- What helps you self-reflect...?

- If you could tell God one thing about your life, what would it be...?

⮑Teen and Parent Conversation
Praying Our Experiences

Share your thoughts with one another based on the following questions.

Teen

- How do you self-reflect (how do you look back over your experiences)?

- What would it be like to spend a day in silence?

- How do you experience life as a Catholic pilgrim?

Parent

- How do you self-reflect (how do you look back over your experiences)?

- How do you find silence in your life?

- Do you have a small community that helps you discern and reflect?

Being a Disciple of Christ: Living Catholicism

Growing up Catholic in a military connected family is a unique experience. As our families participate in the Catholic faith we recognize how our faith connects around the world. We do this whenever we experience mass in a new location. The basic structure of the liturgy is familiar. So are the prayers we pray and hear. Each community is also unique. They possess different gifts. We see these gifts reflected in ministries such as good music or a community that emphasizes reaching out to others in their local neighborhood. We experience it in communities that have a profound sense of prayer which you notice the moment you walk through the door. The Catholic faith is filled with many gifts which we, as members of the community of faith, are called to live into our being.

One of the graces of going to church in military chapels is the opportunity to frequently interact with people of other faiths because we share the same space for prayer. We see a different faith group leaving the chapel as we arrive to participate in the celebration of the Catholic mass. It develops in us a curiosity about other denominations along with a desire to be able to understand why Catholics do the things we do. About 25% of the U.S. military population belongs to the Catholic faith. That means we have a lot of people to share our faith with. It also means that we grow up knowing that people connect with God in a variety of different ways.

It is exciting to be Catholic. Our identity as baptized members of the Catholic Church means that we have put on Christ. In receiving the Eucharist Christ also dwells within us. We reconnect with our believing community and we promise to participate and share in the life of that community. As Catholics we belong. We are a necessary part of a growing community that celebrates the presence of Christ.

The Catholic faith has three important areas that help each of us to live our faith into our very being. They include scripture, the magesterium, and our tradition. Scripture is the word of God we find in the bible. We hear that word broken open on Sundays through the proclamation of the readings and the homilies given by priests and deacons. The magesterium are the people that are the leaders of the church. It includes the pope, our cardinals, bishops, priests and those that teach the faith. Our leaders, guided by the Holy Spirit, serve the community of faith as they seek to understand how Christ is being revealed in the world today. The tradition is the blessing of those who have gone before us in faith. People who have lived and celebrated the Catholic faith over the centuries have passed on their faith to new generations. We receive their tradition, their ways of living the faith, and we also pass it on.

So how do we live our Catholic faith? We look to scripture to see how the people of the old and the new testaments encountered God. We discover how Christ entered the world and who he spent his time with. We look to our leaders to seek guidance in making moral and ethical choices in our daily living.

We learn how our faith strives to make a difference in the lives of the poor and those being neglected. We look to our tradition to see how the faithful lived their faith. We learn about their struggles and their joys. Catholics have a path of faith, a way of life that helps us to express joy and gratitude for the relationships in our lives that matter most.

To be a disciple of Christ means that we strive to always learn and grow. The disciples of Christ followed him wherever he went. The disciples, however, were not just followers. The disciples became students of Christ. They learned what it meant to live a Christian life. It is through being a student of Christ that we also live our faith into our daily existence. A student in a classroom can get by only learning what they need to know to pass a test or make a grade. A student of faith, however, dwells in a deeper reality. What we learn in the Catholic faith becomes incorporated into our very body, our very being. As Catholics we learn skills, ways of being, to develop our spiritual growth. These skills are different than spiritual practices.

...skills, for spiritual growth are not the same as practices. Skills involve the basic tasks or components that make up the broader behavior or practice. Skills are more technical than practices. An example of a spiritual practice is suffering with others, but learning how to show empathy is an example of a skill related to that practice. Confession and reconciliation are examples of spiritual practices, while learning how to obtain a second chance is a related skill. It may be helpful to consider skills for spiritual growth as exercises that contribute to an adolescent's ability and willingness to demonstrate spiritual practices. Moreover, adolescents want these skills.[22]

Skills are the practical ways that we go about living our faith in the real world. These skills remain with us as a way of loving and being in relationship with others throughout our entire life.

We often hear people say that they practice a particular faith. This usually means that they are active in their faith communities and are generally seen as faithful people. Practicing Catholics do more than show up week after week to participate in the celebration of mass. Practicing Catholics develop skills that contribute to the ways in which they live their faith daily. Being Catholic represents a deeper way of identifying ourselves and the relationships in our lives that are important to us.

⮑Reflection Questions
Being a Disciple of Christ

- How do you notice others living their Catholic faith in their daily lives?

- When do you make time to read scripture?

- What have you recently read or learned about the leadership of the church?

- What is a tradition in the church that you identify with?

- In what ways are you a disciple of Christ?

- What are three things about being Catholic that are exciting to you?

- What faith skills do you need to develop? (*see the self assessment rating experience in this reflection*)

⊃Experience
Being a Disciple of Christ

Youth/Parent Exercise

Check out the list of religious, moral and emotional skills on page 116. Spend time with your parent or sponsor going over these lists. Each of you, on a separate piece of paper, are invited to rate yourself on a scale of 1 to 10. A rating of 1 is low and a rating of 10 is high. Go through all three lists and give yourself a rating. The number 10 indicates a skill that you have developed. The number 1 indicates a skill that you have not developed at all. The range of numbers in between indicates a scale so that you can honestly rate where you are right now with regard to each of these skills.

After completing the rating make two of your own lists for each category. The first list you make will include the skills that you think you already have a good handle on. The second list you make will include the skills that you would like or need to develop. Together make a three to six month plan to seek out these skills that you would like to develop. Look for help in your Catholic faith community. Some of the skills require simple conversations to learn. Others skills will require a deeper learning.

For further reading seek out the following two resources written by Michael Carotta which contribute to developing spiritual growth in young people. They include *Sometimes We Dance Sometimes We Wrestle,* 2002 and *Have Faith:*

Sustaining the Spirit for Confirmation and Beyond: A Candidate & Sponsor Resource, 2007. The first is written for adults that parent, mentor, coach or serve young people. The second is written for young people and their sponsors to develop a spiritual plan to live their faith beyond the sacrament of confirmation. Both of these books would be worth reading to continue looking at how we pass on the faith and plan to live it.

⮠Religious, Moral and Emotional Skills.[23]

Rate yourself on the following faith skills,
1=low, 10=high.

Religious faith skills include:

How to recognize God's presence

1 2 3 4 5 6 7 8 9 10

How to pray

1 2 3 4 5 6 7 8 9 10

How to share faith experiences

1 2 3 4 5 6 7 8 9 10

How to apply the Bible to one's own life

1 2 3 4 5 6 7 8 9 10

How to use religious imagination

1 2 3 4 5 6 7 8 9 10

How to participate in communal worship

1 2 3 4 5 6 7 8 9 10

Emotional awareness skills include:

How to stay hopeful

1 2 3 4 5 6 7 8 9 10

How to handle anger

1 2 3 4 5 6 7 8 9 10

How to initiate and accept reconciliation

1 2 3 4 5 6 7 8 9 10

How to handle fear

1 2 3 4 5 6 7 8 9 10

How to practice problem solving

1 2 3 4 5 6 7 8 9 10

How to express affection

1 2 3 4 5 6 7 8 9 10

Moral living skills include:

How to handle sexual and social pressure

1 2 3 4 5 6 7 8 9 10

How to recognize and respond to others in need

1 2 3 4 5 6 7 8 9 10

How to build and maintain healthy relationships
(and terminate unhealthy ones)

1 2 3 4 5 6 7 8 9 10

How to obtain second chances

1 2 3 4 5 6 7 8 9 10

How to handle violence

1 2 3 4 5 6 7 8 9 10

How to analyze society's values and issues

1 2 3 4 5 6 7 8 9 10

How to distinguish between right and wrong

1 2 3 4 5 6 7 8 9 10

➲Teen and Parent Conversation
Being a Disciple of Christ

Share your thoughts with one another based on the following questions.

Teen

- How does being Catholic affect your daily life?

- What is the name of a Catholic person in your community that you admire? Why do admire them?

- What faith skills do you have?

Parent

- How does being Catholic affect your daily life?

- What is the name of a Catholic person you admired when you grew up?

- How have you turned your religious skills into faith practices?

Being Christ for One Another: Serving

While serving as the Catholic youth ministry leader with the U.S. Army in Germany my wife and I were introduced to the Missionaries of Charity in Mannheim. Four missionaries were sent to Mannheim to form a community to serve the poor. These sisters were members of the religious order founded by Mother Teresa. On Saturday afternoons, often with a few teenagers, we would drive through the downtown streets of Mannheim to meet the sisters and others who volunteered to help them. Together, we brought the sisters just a few blocks to a Muslim owned fruit and vegetable store. The owner's of this store allowed us to go into their small warehouse to pick through crates of food that had not sold that week and were on the way to be thrown out. Squatting among the over ripened produce we sorted through what could be salvaged. It was messy work that required lifting, hauling and getting your hands dirty. After an hour or so we brought the sisters and the food back to their residence.

When our cars pulled up there were always people waiting in line. Some of those that were waiting would help us unload the cars and then patiently wait for the sisters to distribute food. The sisters knew everyone in those lines. Part of their mission was to go out into the community and visit those in need. They had spent time in the previous week visiting everyone standing in that line. They knew who had young families or elderly relatives. They knew those that were trying to get more than they could consume. These sisters understood the call to recognize the face of Christ in the people that they served. Their prayer life moved them into direct relationship with those in need.

The Missionaries of Charity spent a great deal of time visiting people. They listened to the stories of the poor. They prayed with them. They invited them to come and receive food. They also welcomed them to special gatherings and celebrations. In the complexity of modern life all around them the sisters relied on the providence of God. God would provide for the needs of those they served. The sisters did their part by being totally present to people that no one else would pay attention to. They also spent a great deal of time in prayer as they pursued a simple way of being. This way of life had its struggles and challenges. Every time we visited, we experienced great joy among those sisters who understood deeply what it meant to be Christ for one another.

Sharing our gifts is a challenge in the world today. Daily life tends to focus on the many ways we ought to take care of ourselves. We see people that strive for status, or seek to be noticed for a job well done. We hear stories of people that go on service projects but only talk about themselves and what they did upon their return. Sometimes, we are those people. We live in-between those that have and those that need. Christian service is a different way of being. It is a true ministry of giving when we move beyond ourselves to serve those in need. As Christians we are called to give the gift of service away without any expectation of some sort of return on our investment of time.

Being Christ for one another is a way of serving so that we recognize the presence of Christ in each person. Sometimes, we are asked to help or do something that we think will make us uncomfortable. It is usually in these times that we gain more than we give. We experience the face of Christ in those without status, or money or prestige. This way of service is a life skill that we are called to practice. Serving without being noticed is different than being humble. It means that in our giving we are called to do so in way that points to Christ, not us. Understanding what it means to be Catholic leads us to move beyond ourselves and our needs. Our gifts are not things that we collect on our pilgrimage to hold on to. Gifts received are meant to be shared.

The Catholic community of faith needs your gifts. The world needs your gifts. You are uniquely created to share the gifts and talents that you have received. Your pilgrimage of faith on the move has brought you into many encounters where you have seen or experienced needs. Our life task is to creatively discern where God is calling us to use the gifts we have been given. We recognize the presence of Christ in those we serve and Christ is seen in us as we lend a hand. When we serve others we truly are being Christ for one another.

⟳Reflection Questions
Being Christ for One Another

- Identify some of your gifts that help you serve others. How have you used them?

- Where have you experienced others really serving the needs of the poor?

- When have others served you?

- When have you served others?

- Did you get to know the people you served or did you serve from afar? Why?

- How can you make time to listen to people in need in your community?

- How does moving around help you recognize needs in different cultures?

➲Experience
Being Christ for One Another

The challenge to go out and listen

When we think of service we tend to think of a project that needs to be taken on or a problem that needs to be solved. Those potential solutions can be helpful. At the root of each of these situations though are people that are deeply affected. If we focus all of our attention on a project and never interact with the person being assisted we miss the chance to see the face of God.

This challenge moves beyond the mini-pilgrimage on page 99 which was designed to help us observe. In your community spend some time praying about who God is calling you to listen to. It might be a friend who has a parent deployed. It might be someone who just moved into the community and is really missing the place that they came from. It might be someone who is pushed aside by others or is often not acknowledged. Reach out to this person and really listen. Don't spend time trading stories or attempting to offer solutions, just listen to their story, to their experience, and to their needs. You might conclude by offering to pray with that person. This ministry of service is about being Christ for one another.

↻Teen and Parent Conversation
Being Christ for One Another

Share your thoughts with one another based on the following questions.

Teen

- What does being Christ for one another mean to you?

- What gifts do you have to share with others?

- How have you shared those gifts with others in the past?

Parent

- What does being Christ for one another mean to you?

- When have others shared their gifts with you?

- How do you decide when and where to share your gifts?

Chapter 4 Notes

[17] Pollock and Van Reken, *Third Culture Kids: The Experience of Growing Up Among Worlds*, 125.

[18] Robert Elsberg, *All Saints: Daily Reflections on Saints, Prophets and Witnesses For Our Time*, (The Crossroad Publishing Company, New York, New York, 2004), 370.

[19] Saint Augustine, translated by Henry Chadwick, *Confessions*, (Oxford University Press, Oxford, England, 1991, reprinted 1992), 3.

[20] Pollack and Van Reken, *Third Culture Kids: The Experience of Growing Up Among Worlds*, 146.

[21] A small group can take many forms. It could be a few close friends, a Catholic youth group or retreat setting, a bible study group or a few people from your Catholic faith community that commit to sharing prayer, experiences and stories with one another. Some of great movements and renewals in the Catholic Church revolve around small group settings.

[22] Michael Carotta, *Sometimes We Dance Sometimes We Wrestle: Embracing the Spiritual Growth of Adolescents*, (Harcourt Religion Publishers, Orlando, Florida, 2002), 56.

[23] Ibid, Carotta, 57. *The following list was compiled by Dr. Michael Carotta.*

Wrapping Up

We began this resource comparing the military connected life with the life of a medieval pilgrim. It seems to be an appropriate analogy for those of us in transition, as Kenda Creasy Dean points out:

Pilgrimages were never undertaken for the sake of the journey itself. Pilgrims traveled with a destination in mind–union with God, symbolized by a liminal experience of "arriving" at a sacred spot. Once arriving, the medieval pilgrim could grasp Christ's Passion emotionally as well as intellectually, having re-imagined Jesus' journey to the cross in order to become a living symbol of Christ's sacrificial love. Then as now, pilgrimages held special appeal for people in transition (especially for those moving from sin to absolution, but also for people in life cycle transitions like adolescence, middle age, or retirement). The spiritual pilgrimage 'moved' these people, quite literally, to explore the profound questions that typically arise in these periods, acknowledging transition itself as part of imitating Christ.[24]

As Catholic pilgrims we have moved through many transitions in our military connected life. Our journey of faith has grown over time and place. It has moved us to dwell deeper in the presence of Christ. It has given us a passion for being excited about living our faith through our daily experiences. Our transitions become a part of imitating Christ because we have been in relationship with him through times of great and difficult change. That intimate relationship calls for a response which is found in our prayer, our participation in the life of the community and through our service to one another. May God bless you as in him you continue to live and move and have your being.

Note

[24] Kenda Creasy Dean, *Practicing Passion: Youth and the Quest For A Passionate Church,* (William B. Eerdmans Publishing Company, Grand Rapids, Michigan, 2004), 204.

Bibliography

Armstrong, Kenneth, Suzanne Best, Paula Domenici, *Courage After Fire: Coping Strategies for Troops Returning from Iraq and Afghanistan and Their Families*, (Ulysses Press, Berkley California, 2006).

Bass, Dorothy C. and Don Richter, editors, *Way to Live: Christian Practices for Teens*, (Upper Room Books, Nashville, Tennessee, 2002).

Blohm, Judith M., *Where in the World Are You Going?*, (Intercultural Press, Inc., Yarmouth, Maine, 1996).

Brown, Raymond, et. al., *The New Jerome Biblical Commentary*, (Prentice Hall, Upper Saddle River, New Jersey, 1990)

Carotta, Michael, *Have Faith: Sustaining the Spirit for Confirmation and Beyond: A Candidate and Sponsor Resource*, (Twenty-Third Publications, New London, Connecticut, 2007).

Carotta, Michael, *Nurturing the Spiritual Growth of Your Adolescent*, (Living Our Faith Series, Harcourt Religion Publishers, Orlando, Florida, 2002).

Carotta, Michael, *Sometimes We Dance Sometimes We Wrestle: Embracing the Spiritual Growth of Adolescents*, (Harcourt Religion Publishers, Orlando, Florida, 2002).

Chadwick, Henry translated Saint Augustine, *Confessions,* (Oxford University Press, Oxford, England, 1991, reprinted 1992).

Dean, Kenda Creasy, *Practicing Passion: Youth and the Quest For A Passionate Church,* (William B. Eerdmans Publishing Company, Grand Rapids, Michigan, 2004).

DeVries, Mark, *Family-Based Youth Ministry: Revised and Expanded,* (Inter Varsity Press, Downers Grove, Illinois, 1994, 2004).

Eidse, Faith and Nina Sichel, editors, *Unrooted Childhoods: Memoirs of Growing up Global,* (Nicholas-Brealey Publishing in Association with Intercultural Press, Yarmouth, Maine, 2004).

Elizondo, Virgilio, *Galilean Journey: The Mexican-American Promise,* (Orbis Books, Maryknoll, New York, 1983, 2000).

Elizondo, Virgilio, *The Future Is Mestizo: Life Where Cultures Meet, Revised Edition,* (University Press of Colorado, Boulder, Colorado, 2000).

Elsberg, Robert, *All Saints: Daily Reflections on Saints, Prophets and Witnesses For Our Time,* (The Crossroad Publishing Company, New York, New York, 2004).

Ender, Morton, *Military Brats and Other Global Nomads: Growing Up in Organization Families,* (Prager Publishers, Westport, Connecticut, 2002).

Hall, Edward T., *Beyond Culture,* (Anchor Books, a division of Random House, Incorporated, New York, New York, 1989).

Killen, Patricia, O'Connell and John De Beer: *The Art of Theological Reflection,* (Crossroad Publishing Company, New York, New York, 1994, 2004).

Klein, Rev. Peter, *The Catholic Source Book* (Third Edition, Brown-ROA, Orlando, Florida, 2000).

Law, Eric H. F., *The Wolf Shall Dwell with the Lamb: A Spirituality for Leadership in a Multicultural Community*, (Chalice Press, St. Louis, Missouri, 1993).

Law, Eric, H. F., *Sacred Acts, Holy Change*, (Chalice Press, St. Louis, Missouri, 2002).

Lee, Marlene, *The Hero in My Pocket*, (Early Light Press, LLC, Boyds, Maryland, 2005).

McCarty, Robert, J., general editor, *The Vision of Catholic Youth Ministry: Fundamentals, Theory and Practice*, (Saint Mary's Press, Winona, Minnesota, 2005).

Parker, Evelyn, *Trouble Don't Last Always: Emancipatory Hope Among African American Adolescents*, (The Pilgrim Press, Cleveland, Ohio, 2003).

Parks, Sharon Daloz, *Big Questions, Worthy Dreams: Mentoring Young Adults in Their Search for Meaning, Purpose and Faith*, (Jossey-Bass, A Wiley Company, San Francisco, California, 2000).

Pavlicin, Karen, *Life After Deployment: Military Families Share Reunion Stories and Advice*, (Elva Resa Publishing, Saint Paul, Minnesota, 2007).

Pollack, David C. and Ruth E. Van Reken, *Third Culture Kids: The Experience of Growing Up Among Worlds*, (Nicholas-Brealey Publishing, Boston, Massachusetts, 1999, 2001).

Robertson, Rachel, *Deployment Journal for Kids*, (Elva Resa Publishing, Saint Paul, Minnesota, 2005).

Roebben, Bert and Michael Warren, *Religious Education as Practical Theology*, (Peeters, Leuven, Belgium, 2001).

Roehlkepartain, Eugene C., *Building Assets in Congregations: A Practical Guide for Helping Youth Grow Up Healthy*, (Search Institute, Minneapolis, Minnesota, 1998).

Simon, Arthur, *How Much is Enough?: Hungering for God in an Affluent Culture*, (Baker Books a division of Baker Book House Company, Grand Rapids, Michigan, 2003).

Smith, Christian and Melinda Lundquist Denton, *Soul Searching: The Religious and Spiritual Lives of American Teenagers*, (Oxford University Press, New York, New York, 2005).

Stoop, David, and Stephanie Arterburn, *The War is Over: But Children Still Have Questions*, (Tyndale House Publishers, Inc., Wheaton, Illinois, 1991).

Vandesteeg, Carol, *When Duty Calls: A Handbook for Families Facing Military Separation*, (Life Journey, Cook Communications Ministries, Colorado Springs, Colorado, 2005).

Voegele, Ben, *We're Moving Where?: An Adolescent's Guide to Overseas Living*, (Millennial Mind Publishing an imprint of American Book Publishing, Salt Lake City, Utah, 2003).

Wertsch, Mary Edwards, *Military Brats: Legacies of Childhood Inside the Fortress*, (Fawcett Publishing, Columbine, New York, 1991).

White, David F., *Practicing Discernment with Youth: A Transformative Youth Ministry Approach*, (The Pilgrim Press, Cleveland, Ohio, 2005).

Additional Resources

Brats: Our Journey Home, A Donna Musil Film, The First Documentary About Growing Up Military, (Brats Without Borders, Eatonton, Georgia, 2005).

The Catholic Youth Bible, New Revised Standard Version, (Saint Mary's Press, Christian Brothers Publications, Winona, Minnesota, 2000).

Chart Your Course: Planning a Successful Journey through High School and Beyond, (Military Child Education Coalition, 2001).

Exit Right, Enter Right: Healthy Cultural Transitions, (Interaction International CD-Rom resource, Colorado Springs, Colorado, 2005).

Go and Make Disciples: A National Plan and Strategy for Catholic Evangelization in the United States, (Tenth Anniversary English and Spanish edition, United States Conference of Catholic Bishops, Washington, D.C., 2002).

General Directory for Catechesis, (United States Catholic Conference, Washington, D.C., 1998, 2001).

How communities can support the children and families of those serving in the National Guard or Reserves, (Military Child Education Coalition, 2004).

Huebner, Ph.D., Angela J. and Jay A. Mancini, Ph.D., *Adjustments among Adolescents in Military Families When a Parent Is Deployed*, (Final

Report to the Military Family Research Institute and Department of Defense Quality of Life Office, June 30, 2005).

National Directory for Catechesis, (United States Conference of Catholic Bishops, Washington, D.C., 2005).

The Princeton Lectures on Youth, Culture and Church, (Princeton Theological Seminary, The Institute for Youth Ministry, 2005).

Renewing the Vision: A Framework for Catholic Youth Ministry, (United States Catholic Conference, Washington, D.C., 1997).

Roman Catholic Sacramentary, (The Catholic Book Publishing Company, Totowa, NJ, 1985).

Welcoming the Stranger Among Us: Unity in Diversity, (A Statement of the U.S. Catholic Bishops, United States Conference of Catholic Bishops, Washington, D.C., 2000, 2001).

Working With Military Children: A Primer for School Personnel, (A project of the Virginia Joint Military Family Services Board, Military Child Education Coalition, 2001).